R. E. Wakefield

New American Home Cook Book

Containing all the most valuable household recipes in the world. The only complete book of its kind. How to make a meal out of nothing. A treasure for rich and poor

R. E. Wakefield

New American Home Cook Book
Containing all the most valuable household recipes in the world. The only complete book of its kind. How to make a meal out of nothing. A treasure for rich and poor

ISBN/EAN: 9783337068776

Printed in Europe, USA, Canada, Australia, Japan

Cover: Foto ©Lupo / pixelio.de

More available books at **www.hansebooks.com**

NEW AMERICAN

HOME COOK BOOK.

CONTAINING

ALL THE MOST VALUABLE HOUSEHOLD RECIPES IN THE WORLD.

THE ONLY COMPLETE BOOK OF ITS KIND.

HOW TO MAKE A MEAL OUT OF NOTHING.

A TREASURE FOR RICH AND POOR.

NEW YORK:
PUBLISHED BY E. G. RIDEOUT & CO., 10 BARCLAY ST.

1881.

INTRODUCTION.

Having secured the services of the distinguished cook and housekeeper, Mrs. R. E. Wakefield, to compile this book, we present it to the American public with the belief that it will be found more valuable than any other work of its kind, and at the same time to retail at the lowest possible figures. We feel certain that upon comparing this valuable little cook book with any other work of the same kind ever published, you will be immediately convinced as to its value. Send for a dozen extra copies at trade prices, and do your utmost to circulate it among your friends. By so doing, you will not only make money for yourself, but confer a lasting benefit upon your fellow creatures.

PUBLISHERS NEW AMERICAN COOK BOOK.

NEW AMERICAN HOME COOK BOOK.

HOW TO CHOOSE MEAT.

BEEF.—Ox beef is the best; is a fine-grained meat. The lean is of a bright red color, intermingled with grains of fat when very good. The fat should be white, not yellow, and the suet white and firm. Bull fat is dark colored and coarse grained, and should be avoided. Beef should not be lean, for if it is so, it is tough and bad.

The rib or sirloin is the best for roasting. Take care to have your sirloin cut from the slim end. Epicures prefer the rump, but it is too large for small families, and we wish to treat of household dishes only.

VEAL should be small and white, the flesh dry and closely grained. Veal makes good stock for rich soups.

MUTTON should be dark colored, and have plenty of fat. The older mutton is, the better it is. The saddle is the best; the haunch next. The legs and loin separated are the best joints after the haunch.

LAMB should be small, of a pale red color, and fat.

PORK.—The fat of pork should be firm, and the lean white and finely grained; the rind thin and smooth.

BACON.—The rind should be thin, the fat firm and pinkish, the lean tender and fast to the bone.

TO TEST A HAM.—Stick a small knife into it up to the knuckle. If, when drawn out, it has a nice smell, the ham is good; if otherwise, reject it.

VENISON.—Test in the same manner as a ham. The fat should be thick and clean. If the cleft of the haunch is smooth and close, the animal is young.

TO CHOOSE GAME AND POULTRY

FOWLS.—A young rooster has a smooth leg and short spur; vent close and dark. Young hens have smooth legs and combs. A good capon has a thick belly and large rump.

TURKEY.—The male bird, when young, has a smooth black leg and short spur; eyes bright and full, and feet supple. The hen may be judged in the same manner.

DUCKS.—In young ducks the feet and bills will be yellow and free from hair. When fresh, the feet are pliable; they are stiff when stale.

GEESE may be selected by the same rules.

PIGEONS should have supple feet and firm vents. If discolored, reject them.

PARTRIDGES.—Yellow legs and dark bills are the best signs by which a young bird may be known; a rigid vent when fresh.

RABBITS.—A young, fresh rabbit should have a stiff body, the cleft in the lip narrow, the claws smooth and sharp.

GROUSE, WOODCOCK, SNIPE, QUAIL, &c., may be chosen by the above rules. Buy a white-legged fowl for boiling, and a dark-legged one for roasting.

TO CHOOSE FISH.

FRESH FISH should have bright eyes, clear, red gills, stiff body, and smell fresh.

SALMON AND COD should have a small head, thick shoulders, and a small tail. The flesh of salmon should be bright red, scales bright.

EELS should be bought alive.

CRABS AND LOBSTERS should be heavy and very stiff.

TO CHOOSE EGGS.

If the eggs rattle when shaken, they are bad. The best plan is to put them in a basin of water, and see if they lie on their side; should the egg turn upon its end, it is bad.

THE KITCHEN.

LENTILS IN THE GERMAN WAY.

Soak the lentils—the whole ones—for twelve hours, then put them in a saucepan, and well cover with meat stock, boil for three hours, then add a pat of butter and a little flour and vinegar according to taste.

SHRIMP SOUP.

Take one pint of shrimps, and pound them in a mortar with the juice of half a lemon and a piece of butter equal in weight to them. When quite a smooth paste, pass it through a sieve, and add pepper, salt and grated nutmeg. Take as much breadcrumbs as there is shrimp pulp, and soak in stock; melt a piece of butter in a saucepan, amalgamate with it a heaped tablespoonful of flour, mix the shrimp pulp with the bread crumbs, and put both into the saucepan; stir well, and add more stock until a *purée* is obtained rather thinner in consistency than the soup should be. Put the saucepan on the fire, stir the contents till they thicken and boil, draw it then on one side, carefully skim off the superfluous fat, strain the soup through a hair sieve, make it boiling hot, and serve.

A WINTER RELISH.

Take a calf's or sheep's heart and liver, stuff the heart with forcemeat, and roast it before the fire till done; take the liver, cut it in slices, and fry it; take some gravy and a little melted butter, to which add a little cayenne, salt, ketchup and India soy to taste. Put the liver round the heart on your dish, and pour the gravy over them. Have ready rolled bacon and crisped parsley to garnish.

ANGEL PUDDING.

Two ounces of flour, two ounces of powdered sugar, two ounces of butter melted in half a pint of new milk, two eggs; mix well. Bake the above in small patty-pans until nicely browned, and send to table on a dish covered with a serviette. A little powdered sugar should be sifted over each pudding, and slices of lemon served with them. The eggs must be well beaten before they are added to the other ingredients.

CREAM DRESSING.

When oil is disliked in salads, the following dressing will be found excellent: Rub the yolks of two hard-boiled eggs very fine with a spoon, incorporate with them a dessertspoonful of mixed mustard; then stir in a tablespoonful of melted butter, half a teacupful of thick cream, a saltspoonful of salt, and cayenne pepper enough to take up on the point of a very small penknife-blade, and a few drops of anchovy or Worcestershire sauce, and, very carefully, sufficient vinegar to reduce the mixture to a smooth creamy consistency, and pour it upon lettuce carefully prepared for the table.

CRUMPETS.

Mix a quart of good milk with water to make a batter, add a little salt, an egg, and a teaspoonful of good yeast; beat well, cover up, and let it stand in a warm place to rise. Clean the muffin plate, or, not having this, a frying pan, while warm over the fire, and rub it with a greased cloth, or a little butter tied up in a piece of muslin; pour a cupful of the batter into the pan or on the plate; as it begins to bake, raise the edge all round with a sharp knife. When one side is done, turn and bake the other side. Crumpets are generally now poured into proper sized rings of tin, which makes them all of a size and thickness. A little rye flour is an improvement.

FOWL SCOLLOPS.

Strip off the skin from a cold roast or boiled fowl, cut the meat into thin slices, and warm them in about half-pint or rather more of bechamel, or white sauce. Serve quite hot, and garnish the dish with rolled ham or bacon toasted.

TO RAGOUT A DUCK WHOLE.

After having emptied and singed a duck, season it inside with pepper and salt, and truss it. Roast it before a clear fire for twenty minutes, and let it acquire a nice brown color. Put it into a stew pan with sufficient well-seasoned beef gravy to cover it, slice and fry two onions, and add these with sage leaves and lemon thyme, both of which should be finely minced, to the stock. Simmer gently until the duck is tender; strain, skim and thicken the gravy with a little butter and flour, boil it up, pour over the duck, and serve. One and a half pints of young peas when in season, added to the gravy, improves the ragout immensely.

TO DRESS A LOBSTER.

Take the flesh of a lobster, and chop it very fine; add some gravy, chopped shallots, parsley, cayenne pepper, and salt to your taste; stew it in a stew pan; then put it into the shells and some crumbs of bread over it, and clarified butter; then brown it with a salamander. The shells of the body cut in half, and the two half-shells of the tail.

SPONGE BISCUITS.

Beat the yolks of twelve eggs for half an hour, then put in one and a half pounds of beaten sifted sugar, and whisk it till it rises in bubbles; beat the whites to a strong froth, and whisk them well with the sugar and yolks, work in fourteen ounces of flour, with the rinds of two lemons grated. Bake them in tin moulds buttered, in a quick oven, for an hour; before they are baked, sift a little fine sugar over them.

SPONGE CAKE.

Pare a good-sized lemon thin, put the peeling into a quarter of a pint of water, let it stand some hours. When about to make the cake, put three-quarters of a pound of sugar into a saucepan, pour the water and peel upon it, and let it stand by the fire to get hot. Break eight eggs into a deep earthen vessel that has been made quite hot; whisk the eggs for a few minutes with a whisk that has been dipped in hot water; make the sugar and water boil up, and pour it boiling hot over the eggs; continue to whisk them briskly for a quarter of an hour; have one pound of flour well dried and quite warm from the fire; just stir it lightly in. Put the cake into tins lined with white paper, and bake them immediately in a moderately hot oven

SPRUCE BEER.

Although this beverage is known under the name of *beer*, it is, in fact, a wine as much as many others that are acknowledged as such. It is of two kinds, brown and white. The latter is by far preferable, and is made as follows: Take seven pounds of the cheapest loaf sugar; dissolve it in four and a half gallons of hot water. When the temperature has fallen to blood heat, mix in about four ounces of essence of spruce, and dissolve it perfectly by agitation; then add half a pint of good solid yeast from a brewery, and mix thoroughly. A fermentation will soon commence, which, if it be summer, will rapidly go through its stages; but if in winter, must be maintained by keeping the cask in a warm apartment. When the fermentation very perceptibly subsides, the liquor is to be drawn off, the cask well washed, and the liquor returned. A second fermentation, inconsiderable in degree, will take place, and when this diminishes, the liquor is fit for bottling. The bottles should be wired down, and laid on their sides until the liquor becomes brisk, and in high order. This will be known by the trial of a bottle; and it then becomes prudent to set the bottles on their end, lest they should burst. When kept too long in this posture, the beer is apt to become flat, in which case the bottles must be placed on their sides again. Brown spruce beer may be made exactly according to the same formula, except that in place of white sugar an equal weight of molasses or treacle is to be made use of.

TO RESTORE SOUR MILK OR CREAM.

Milk or cream, when it has turned sour, may be restored to its original sweetness by means of a small quantity of carbonate of magnesia. When the acidity is slight, half a teaspoonful of the powder to a pint of milk.

LOBSTER BALLS.

Take the meat of a lobster with the coral and spawn, pound in a mortar, add bread crumbs, about a quarter the proportion of the lobster, and season with cayenne, white pepper, mace and salt. Mix sufficient melted butter with the whole to form into a mass, make into balls the size of small apples, egg well, dip in bread crumbs, and fry a pale brown.

TO CANDY FRUIT.

After peaches, plums, citrons or quinces have been preserved, take the fruit from the syrup; drain it on a sieve; to a pound of loaf sugar put half a teacup of water; when it is dissolved, set it over a moderate fire; when boiling hot, put in the fruit; stir it continually until the sugar is candied about it; then take it upon a sieve, and dry it in a warm oven, or before a fire; repeat this two or three times if you wish.

PEAR MARMALADE.

To six pounds of small pears take four pounds of sugar; put the pears into a saucepan with a little cold water; cover it, and set it over the fire until the fruit is soft, then put them into cold water; pare, quarter and core them; put to them three teacups of water, set them over the fire; roll the sugar fine, mash the fruit fine and smooth, put the sugar to it, stir it well together until it is thick like jelly; then put it into tumblers or jars, and when it is quite cold, secure it in the same way as jelly.

TO PRESERVE BUTTER.

Melt it in an earthen vessel, surrounded with warm water. Skim the butter until clear, and pour the pure portion off into pots, which should be filled to the top and closely covered. A little salt may be added before pouring, and should be stirred in, afterwards allowing the butter to clear. Or mix two ounces of salt with one ounce each of saltpetre and white sugar. Add one ounce of this mixture, in fine powder, to each pound of butter, working it well in. The butter must not be used for a month, and the pots containing it must be filled to the brim.

BLACKBERRY JAM.

Gather the fruit in dry weather; allow half a pound of good brown sugar to every pound of fruit; boil the whole together gently for an hour, or till the blackberries are soft, stirring and mashing them well. Preserve it like any other jam, and it will be found very useful in families, particularly for children. It may be spread on bread instead of butter; and even when the blackberries are bought, it is cheaper than butter. In the country every family should preserve at least half a peck of blackberries.

A VERY GOOD PLAIN CAKE.

Rub eight ounces of butter into two pounds of flour; mix it with three teaspoonfuls of yeast, which must not be bitter; work it to a paste. Let it rise before the fire for an hour and a half, then mix in the whites and yolks of four eggs, beaten apart, one pound of sugar, three parts of a pint of milk, a glass of raisin wine, the grated rind of a lemon, and a small teaspoonful of pounded ginger. You may add currants or carraway seed, whichever may be preferred.

SPINACH.

Have a pot of boiling water, add salt, and to each gallon of water a small teaspoonful of carbonate of ammonia; when boiled tender, and carefully dried and chopped fine, put in a saucepan, adding butter or sweet oil to taste, with pepper, salt, a very little sugar, and the juice of a lemon. May be served on toast, thin buttered, and poached eggs over it that have been dropped in water to which a little vinegar has been added, or served plain, with hard-boiled eggs sliced and quartered.

SALAD DRESSING.

One teaspoonful of made mustard, one teaspoonful of sugar, two tablespoonfuls of salad oil, four tablespoonfuls of milk, two of vinegar, cayenne pepper and salt to taste. Put the mustard into a salad bowl with the sugar, and add the oil drop by drop, carefully stirring and mixing all the ingredients well together. Proceed in this manner with the milk and vinegar, which must be added very gradually or the sauce will curdle; then put in the seasoning of cayenne and salt. It ought to have a creamy appearance, and when mixing, the ingredients cannot be added too gradually, or stirred too much.

ICE CREAM.

About half fill the icing pot with the mixture which it is desired to freeze, place it in a pail or any suitable wooden vessel, with ice beat small, and mixed with about half its weight of common salt; turn it backwards and forwards as quickly as possible, and as the ice cream sticks to the sides, break it down with an ice spoon, that the whole may be equally exposed to the cold. As the salt and ice in the tub melt, add more, until the process is finished, then put the cream into glasses, and place them in a mixture of salt and ice until wanted for use. Before sending them to the table, dip the outside of the glass into lukewarm water, and wipe it dry. Flavored ice creams are made by mixing "cream for icing" with half its weight of mashed or preserved fruit, previously rubbed through a clean hair sieve; or, when the flavor depends on the juice of fruit or on essential oil, by adding a sufficient quantity of such substances. Thus raspberry and strawberry ice creams are made according to the former method; lemon, orange, noyeau, and almond ice creams, by the latter method. The "cream for icing" is thus made: New milk, two pints; yolks of six eggs; white sugar, four ounces; mix, strain, heat gently and cool gradually. Let it be borne in mind that in icing there ought to be holes at the bottom of the icing pail, to allow the water to run off as the ice melts.

PEACH ICE CREAM.

Break up a dozen ripe peaches, and boil them in a gill of water for ten minutes. Add a small pot of red currant jelly, and when it is dissolved put the peaches through a fine hair sieve; add syrup to give the required sweetness, a few drops of home-made extract of almonds, and a little lemon juice. This, when cold, with an equal quantity of custard or thick cream.

TO KEEP EGGS FRESH.

Three pounds of quicklime, ten ounces of salt, one ounce of cream of tartar, and a gallon and a half of boiling water. Mix the ingredients, stir, and cover close. The eggs may be covered with the solution the following day. They will keep long, but the shell becomes very brittle. The best time for preserving eggs is from July to September.

POTTED HERRING.

Scrape and wash a dozen fish; lay them in salt for three hours; take an earthen jar, and cut the pieces so as to fit the jar; season with a teaspoonful of salt, twenty whole peppers, ten cloves, two bits of mace, and half a teaspoonful of ground ginger; put the fish in layers, adding the salt and spices on each layer; pack down tightly, then fill the jar with three-quarters of vinegar and one-quarter of water; cover the top with a stiff crust of flour and water; bake gently for five hours; eat cold.

HASHED CALF'S HEAD.

The head must be boiled about two hours the night before it is required; or you may, if convenient, use the cold remains of one partly used at table before. Cut the meat carefully into small pieces, and flour each piece a little; then put some butter and flour in a stewpan over the fire, stirring the butter with a wooden spoon till it turns quite brown. Then add about a pint and a half of good gravy, an onion cut very fine, a bunch of sweet herbs tied up in muslin, and a glass of sherry. Let this stew about five minutes, and then add your meat, seasoning it with cayenne and salt, and squeezing in the juice of half a lemon. Garnish with egg or forcemeat balls.

RIZ À L'IMPÉRATRICE.

Boil three tablespoonfuls of rice in a pint of milk, with sugar and vanilla to taste. When done, put in a basin to get cold. Then make a custard with a gill of milk and the yolks of four eggs; when cold mix it with the rice. Whip to a froth a gill of cream, with some sugar and a pinch of gelatine dissolved in a little water. Mix this lightly with the rice and custard, fill a mould with the mixture and set it on ice. When moderately iced, turn it out and serve.

DELICIOUS BEVERAGES.

Iced tea and coffee are delicious beverages. Tea, when it is to be thus used, is best if steeped for a few hours in cold water, having it strong enough to be weakened with ice water when it is served. Or, if hot water is used, it should be steeped but a short time, and then be poured off the leaves; otherwise it will have a rank flavor. Iced tea is usually preferred without cream. Coffee is very nice if cream is added when it is hot, and then it is cooled and iced. Sugar may be added also when it is hot, if the taste of those who are to drink it is well understood; but too much sugar will spoil the coffee for many persons.

MILK LEMONADE.

Dissolve three-quarters of a pound of loaf sugar in one pint of boiling water, and mix with them one gill of lemon juice and one gill of sherry; then add three gills of cold milk. Stir the whole well together, and strain it.

TO BOIL SPINACH.

Boil in plenty of water, drain and press the moisture from it between two trenchers; chop it small, put it into a saucepan with a slice of fresh butter, and stir the whole until well mixed. Smooth it in a dish, and send to table.

CHOCOLATE ICE CREAM.

Mix two teaspoonfuls of cocoa in a gill of cold milk, stir into a pint of cream or custard, add vanilla flavor, and sweeten. Scraped and sifted chocolate, so as to bring it to a fine powder, can be used, but the cocoa is on all accounts best for this cream.

HARDBAKE, OR EVERTON TOFFIE.

Into a brass skillet put a quarter of a pound of fresh butter; as soon as it has just melted, add a pound of brown sugar; keep these stirred very gently over a clear fire till a little of the mixture, dropped into cold water, breaks between the teeth without sticking to them. When it has boiled to this point, it must be poured out immediately, or it will burn. The grated rind of a lemon, added when the toffie is half done, improves it; or else a teaspoonful of powdered ginger, moistened with a little of the other ingredients, so soon as the sugar is dissolved, and then stirred into the whole. If dropped upon a buttered dish, the toffie can, when cold, be raised from it easily. Almonds can be mixed with it, if liked, during the process of stirring.

TO PURIFY WATER.

Pounded alum possesses the property of purifying water. A large teaspoonful of pulverized alum sprinkled into a hogshead of water, (the water stirred round at the time,) will, after the lapse of a few hours, by precipitating to the bottom the impure particles, so purify it, that it will be found to possess nearly all the freshness and clearness of pure spring water. A pailful, containing four gallons, may be purified by a single teaspoonful.

HARE SOUP.

Skin and paunch a fresh-killed hare, then cut it in pieces. Put into a stewpan one pound gravy beef, a slice of ham, one carrot, a faggot of savory herbs, two onions, a quarter of an ounce of whole pepper, a little browned flour, the crumbs of two

French rol's, a quarter of a pint of port wine, a little salt and cayenne; the hare cut into pieces. Add three quarts of water, and simmer gently for eight hours. It must be strained through a sieve, and the best parts of the hare should be put into the soup when served. These pieces must be taken out after about three hours' simmering, and put in to heat again after the soup is strained.

BRILLA SOUP.

Take four pounds shin of beef, and cut all the meat from the bone in nice square pieces, and boil the bone for four hours. Strain the liquor, let it cool and take off the fat; then put the pieces of meat in the cold liquor, cut small three carrots, two turnips and a head of celery; chop two onions, and add them with a large sprig of thyme and seasoning; simmer till the meat is tender, and then color with browning.

LARK PIE.

Make a stuffing of bread-crumbs, parsley, lemon-peel, and the yolk of an egg; roll the larks in flour and stuff them. Line the bottom of a pie-dish with a few slices of beef and bacon; over these place the larks, and season with salt, pepper, minced parsley and chopped chalots. Pour in the stock or water, cover with a crust, and bake for an hour; serve quickly, as it must be hot.

TO KEEP PEARS FOR WINTER USE.

Place the pears, stalks upwards, on a deal shelf, in a dry, but not warm place; do not let them touch one another, and give them plenty of air. In store-houses on purpose for keeping fruit, the shelves are usually composed of a series of battens, so that the fruit rests on the edges of them, where they do not join, and so is surrounded by air, and scarcely touches the wood on which it stands. Where space is an object, apples and pears are frequently kept on layers of straw.

SWEET OMELET.

Six eggs, a tablespoonful of flour, a little sugar, nutmeg, preserve. Beat the eggs very light, add the flour, sugar, and a little nutmeg; put this into an omelet-pan, stir till it sets; loosen the edge with a knife, spread over it with a spoon any kind of preserve.; roll it up quickly and slip on to the serving-dish; sift on a little fine sugar.

TO MASH TURNIPS.

After having been boiled very tender and the water pressed thoroughly from them, put them into a saucepan, and stir constantly for some minutes over a gentle fire; add a little cream, salt, fresh butter and pepper; continue to simmer and stir them for five minutes longer, and then serve them.

BARLEY WATER.

Wipe very clean, by rolling it in a soft cloth, two tablespoonfuls of pearl barley; put it into a quart jug, with a lump or two of sugar and a grain or two of salt; fill up the jug with boiling water, and keep the mixture gently stirred for some minutes; then cover it down and let it stand until perfectly cold. In twelve hours, or less, it would be fit for use. After the barley water has been poured off once, the jug may be filled with boiling water a second time, and even a third time with advantage. If not unpalatable to the invalid, a strip of lemon peel, cut thin, may be added. A glass of calf's-feet jelly is a great improvement.

SCOTCH MARMALADE.

Take some bitter oranges, and double their weight of sugar; cut the rind of the fruit into quarters and peel it off, and if the marmalade be not wanted very thick, take off some of the spongy white skin inside the rind. Cut the chips as thin as possible, and about half an inch long, and divide the pulp into small bits, removing carefully the seeds, which may be steeped in part of the water that is to make the marmalade, and which must be in the proportion of one quart to one pound of fruit. Put the chips and pulp into a deep earthen dish, and pour the water boiling over them; let them remain for twelve or fourteen hours, and then turn the whole into the preserving pan, and boil it until the chips are perfectly tender. When they are so, add by degrees the sugar (which should be previously pounded), and boil the marmalade until it jellies. The water in which the seeds have been steeped, and which must be taken from the quantity apportioned to the whole of the preserve, should be poured into a hair sieve, and the seeds well worked into it with the back of a spoon; a strong, clear jelly will be obtained by these means, which must be washed off them by pouring their own liquor through the sieve in small portions over them. This must be added to the fruit when it is first set on the fire.

SPANISH FRITTERS.

Spanish fritters are a simple and generally popular sweet with young people, and most inexpensive. Take a two-penny roll and cut it into six rounds. Soak in as much milk as they will absorb—about half a pint; brush each round over with whipped egg—one is sufficient—and fry them a bright brown in just as much butter as will cook them without burning. Spread jam of any kind you happen to have, sandwich fashion; between each two rounds sift ground white sugar very lightly over the top. Arrange in any fanciful shape, and serve on a small napkin.

POT CHEESE.

One pound of cheese must be well beaten in a mortar, and to it must be added two ounces of liquid butter, one glass of sherry and a very small quantity of cayenne pepper, mace and salt. All should be well beaten together and be put into a pretty shaped glass potting-jar, with a layer of butter at the top. It makes a delicious relish for bread or toast.

BOILED EELS.

Skin, clean and properly wash a large eel and cut off the head, lay it round and round on a fish-plate, with a little salt, and boil in a very little water. Serve it with parsley and butter.

CRIMPED COD.

Lay a cod in spring water, then cut it up and put into a kettle of water, add two handfuls of salt, and let it boil. Cut the cod into slices two inches thick, take them out with great care not to break them. When they are quite dry, flour them and broil with the gridiron far above the fire. Serve with shrimp or oyster sauce.

PHEASANT CUTLETS.

Prepare three young pheasants in the usual way; cut them into joints and bone them; put the bones into a stew-pan with a little stock herbs, vegetables and seasoning, to make a gravy. Flatten and trim the cutlets, then broil them over a good fire, pile on a dish, and pour under them the gravy; one bone should be placed on the top of each cutlet.

HASHED GAME.

Cut the remains of cold game into joints, reserve the pieces, and the inferior ones and trimmings put into a stew-pan with an onion, pepper, a strip of lemon peel, salt and water or weak stock; stew these for about an hour and strain the gravy; thicken it with butter and flour, add one glass of port wine, one tablespoonful of lemon juice, one tablespoonful of ketchup; lay in the pieces of game, and let them gradually warm through by the side of the fire—they must not boil. Serve and garnish with sippets of toasted bread.

CROCCANTE.

Take half a pound of blanched and finely-chopped sweet almonds, half a pound of loaf sugar, one tablespoonful of essence of lemon, a piece of butter the size of a walnut; boil in a saucepan until it sets—about fifteen or twenty minutes—turn into a flat shape to set. To be eaten cold.

FRIED PLUM PUDDING.

Cut some rather thick slices from a plum pudding, fry them in butter just long enough to warm them, and serve with the following sauce over: Beat the yolks of two eggs, add two tablelpoonfuls of sifted sugar, two of sherry, and two of brandy; mix all well together, put them into a saucepan, and stir over the fire till the mixture thickens.

COFFEE ICE CREAM.

Make a custard, without any flavor, of a pint of cream and four yolks of eggs. Put into this a quarter of a pound of freshly-roasted Mocha coffee berries; they should, if possible, be used hot. Cover up the stew pan closely with its lid, putting a napkin over to keep in the steam. Let the custard stand for an hour, strain and sweeten, and when cold put it into the freezing pot. Cream thus prepared will not take the color of the coffee, and when carefully made is very delicate and delicious. Coffee ice cream is also made with a strong infusion of coffee. To make the infusion, put two ounces of ground coffee into a French cafetière, and pour over it a gill of fast boiling water. When the infusion has all run through boil it up, and pour over it two more ounces of coffee. Put the infusion thus obtained to a pint of sweetened cream or custard and freeze.

OLIVES OF CALF'S HEAD.

Parboil the half of a calf's head with the tongue and brains, and cut even, thin slices from the thickest part of the head, and lengthwise slices from the tongue. Make a stuffing of minced ham, savory herbs, and pepper and salt. Brush the slices with the beaten yolk of an egg, and spread your stuffing equally over them. Roll them firmly into shape, and tie them securely with twine. Lay the olives as closely together as possible in a stew-pan which will just hold them, and stew them very slowly for an hour and a half, with sufficient good stock to nearly cover them, and slices of fat bacon over them. When done, arrange them neatly on a dish with either brown mushroom sauce or the following: Take some strong beef stock, and thicken it with a little butter and flour kneaded together, and two tablespoonfuls of bread crumbs which have been soaked with a little cold new milk. Scald a dozen sage leaves and an equal bulk of parsley, chop these finely, and add them to the sauce, and lastly the brains, cut in small pieces. Serve as hot as possible.

ORANGE TARTS.

Grate a little of the outside of an orange, squeeze the juice into a dish, put the peel into water, and change it often for four days, then put it into a sauce-pan of boiling water on the fire; change the water twice to take out the bitterness, and when tender wipe and beat them fine in a mortar. Boil their weight in double refined sugar into a syrup and skim it; then put in the pulp and boil all together till clear. When cold put it into the tarts, squeeze in the juice, and bake them in a quick oven. Conserve of orange makes good tarts.

ROAST TURKEY.

Fill the inside with stuffing of pork sausage meat, and tie the skin of the neck over the back with stout string. Put a piece of buttered paper over the breast. Place the bird on the spit, and set it at some distance from the fire. Baste it frequently with butter melted in the dripping pan, and flour it occasionally. When nearly done take off the paper and dredge it with flour. Serve it with brown gravy poured over it, and garnish with forcemeat balls. Bread sauce.

POTTED FOWL.

Take the meat from the bones of a cold roast fowl, weigh it, and to every pound add one-quarter of a pound of fresh butter, one teaspoonful of pounded mace, half a small nutmeg, salt and cayenne to taste; cut the meat into small pieces and pound it well with fresh butter; sprinkle in the spices gradually, and keep pounding until reduced to a perfectly smooth paste. Put it into potting-pots for use, and cover with clarified butter about half an inch in thickness, and, if to be kept for some time, tie over a bladder; two or three slices of ham minced and pounded with the above will be found an improvement. It should be kept in a dry place. This makes a very nice breakfast or luncheon dish.

FIG PUDDING.

Chop one-half pound of figs very finely, mix them with one-quarter pound coarse sugar, a tablespoonful of treacle for a tablespoonful of milk, one-half pound flour, one-quarter pound suet, an egg, and a pinch of grated nutmeg. Put the pudding into a buttered mould, and boil for four or five hours.

"GOOD LUCK" PUDDING.

Put into a basin one-quarter pound flour, one-quarter pound chopped suet, one-quarter pound currants, one-quarter pound raisins, one tablespoonful of moist sugar, half teaspoonful of ground ginger, half saltspoonful of salt; mix well with a clean knife; dip the pudding-cloth into boiling water, wring it out, and put in the mixture. Have ready a sauce pan of boiling water, plunge in the pudding, and boil for three hours.

THE EPICURE'S PUDDING.

Make some rich but very light puff paste and line a pie-dish with it. Take one ounce candied lemon peel, the same of orange and citron, and slice it all up in fine, small shavings, laying them at the bottom of the dish, and strewing lightly over them one-half ounce sweet almonds, finely chopped with three or four bitter ones, all previously blanched. Beat the yolks of eight and the whites of two eggs, and mix with one-half pound powdered loaf sugar and a tablespoonful of French brandy. Pour this over the sliced peel, and bake it in a moderately-heated oven for one hour.

GENEVA WAFERS.

Well whisk two eggs; put them into a basin and stir to them three ounces butter, which must be beaten to a cream; add three ounces flour and sifted sugar gradually, and then mix all well together. Butter a baking sheet, and drop on it a teaspoonful of the mixture at a time, leaving a space between each. Bake in a cool oven; watch the pieces of paste, and when half done, roll them up like wafers, and put in a small wedge of bread or piece of wood to keep them in shape; place them in the oven again until crisp. Before serving, remove the bread; put a spoonful of preserve in the widest end and fill up with whipped cream.

CHICKEN JELLY.

Take the leg of a fowl, and, after skinning and scalding it, remove all fat and wash it clean in cold water; then put it into a saucepan, with one breakfast-cupful of water, and salt to taste; boil slowly to pieces, strain into a cup, or let it stand till jellied.

POTATOES À LA LYONNAISE.

Slice an onion finely, and fry it in butter till it begins to take color; add four or five cold boiled potatoes cut in slices three-eighths of an inch thick, salt and pepper to taste, and keep shaking the saucepan till they are quite hot and also begin to brown. Beef dripping, if properly clarified, may be used instead of butter.

BREAD-AND-BUTTER PUDDING.

Butter your pie-dish well, and strew the bottom with currants and candied peel; then place alternate layers of bread and butter in rather thin slices, and the peel and currants, until the dish is nearly full, observing to have currants at the top; then pour over, slowly and equally, a custard of sweetened milk and two or three eggs, flavored to taste, and bake in a moderate oven for about twenty minutes.

DUTCH ROLLS.

Sift three quarts of flour, break three eggs into a pint of cold milk, in which put a teaspoonful of yeast, and stir up; cut up two onnces butter and work it in your flour; mix the milk, eggs and yeast with the flour, knead thoroughly. Make into rolls, butter the pan, and stand by the stove to rise. Bake in a quick oven.

WHITE WINE WHEY.

This is a drink that is used to cause perspiration, in cases of colds or other ailments, where there is no inflammatory tendency in the patient. Take half a pint of milk, and put it on the fire in a sauce-pan, and immediately that it boils put into it two glasses of white wine, with a little sugar dissolved in it. A light floating curd will be instantly seen. Boil for a few minutes; pour it through a hair sieve, so that the whey may run from the curd. Serve the whey hot. Throw away the curd, for it is exceedingly indigestible, and should not be eaten.

POTTED CHICKEN.

Boil the chicken in as little water as possible, till very tender and well done; season, while boiling, to suit the taste; then, while hot, separate the white meat from the dark, and chop both very fine; place the white part in a dish, in any design wanted, as a cross; fill up with the dark meat; pour over it enough of the liquid left in the kettle to thoroughly moisten it; then place a small board over it, and press with heavy weights; after a few hours, turn it out on a platter, and you will have a dish for the table that will be not only delicious, but an ornament.

HAM WITH CURRANT JELLY.

Put half a glass of currant jelly, a small bit of butter, and a little pepper into your sauce-pan; slice boiled ham very thin, and when the jelly is hot put in the ham and leave it only long enough to be heated through. Serve on a hot dish.

IRISH STEW.

Take about two pounds of chops from a loin of mutton, place them in a stew-pan with alternate layers of sliced potatoes and layers of chops, and three small onions, and pour in a pint and a half of cold water; cover the stew-pan closely, and let it stew gently until the potatoes are ready to mash, and the greater part of the gravy is absorbed; then place it in a dish, and serve it very hot.

GRAVY FOR A ROAST FOWL.

Boil the neck of the fowl, after having cut it small, in half a pint of water, with a seasoning of spice or herbs; let it stew very softly for an hour and a half. When the bird is just ready for table, take the gravy from the dripping-pan and drain off the fat; strain the liquor from the neck into it, mixing them smoothly; pass the gravy again through the strainer, heat it, add seasoning if necessary, and take it hot to table.

MINCEMEAT.

Take seven pounds of currants, well picked and cleaned; of finely-chopped beef suet, the lean of a sirloin of beef minced raw, and finely-chopped apples—Kentish golden pippins—each three and a half pounds; citron, lemon peel, and orange peel, cut fine, each half a pound; fine moist sugar, two pounds; mixed spice, an ounce; the rind of four lemons and four Seville oranges; mix well, and put in a deep pan. Mix a bottle of brandy and white wine, and the juice of the lemons and oranges that have been grated, together in a basin; pour half over, and press down tight with the hand, then add the other half and cover closely. Some families make this one year so as to use it the next. Of course, the ingredients may be halved or quartered according to the quantity required.

TO BROWN FLOUR.

Spread it upon a tin plate set upon the stove, or in a very hot oven, and stir continuously after it begins to color until it is brown all through. Keep it in a glass jar, covered closely, and it will always be ready for use.

COLLARED SPROUTS.

Pick over carefully, lay in cold water, slightly salted, for an hour, shake in a colander to drain, and put it into boiling water, keeping at a fast boil until tender. A piece of pork seasons them pleasantly, but in this case put the meat on first, adding the sprouts when parboiled, and cooking them together. Boil in an uncovered vessel, drain very well, chop and heap in a dish, laying the meat on top.

HOW TO BROWN BUTTER.

This is a very simple recipe, but a very useful one. Put a

lump of butter into a frying-pan according to the amount of gravy desired. When it is melted, dredge browned flour over it, and stir to a smooth batter until it begins to boil. Use it to color gravies, and, in fact, it can be made into a sauce, or almost anything; and if the sauce is required to be strong and good, celery, onion, vinegar, brown sugar, cayenne, or a glass of wine may be added, but that will be according to the purpose it is required for.

STEWED TURNIPS.

Cut some new turnips into quarters, put them into a sauce-pan with a piece of butter, give them a toss or two on the fire, then pour in enough stock to cover them; add pepper and salt to taste, and a pinch of sugar, also a little grated nutmeg, and let them stew slowly till done.

ITALIAN BEEF OLIVES (BRACCIOLETTE.)

Take a piece of fillet of beef, remove all fat and gristle, and mince it finely, mixing with it salt, one or two cloves, powdered, and a little oil and chopped fat bacon, sweet herbs and parsley to taste. When well amalgamated, roll it out and divide it into small pieces; form each piece into an olive, roll them in liquefied butter and then in fine bread crumbs. Just before they are wanted, broil at a good fire, first on one side, then on the other. If done too long, they will be spoiled.

CHRISTMAS PLUM PUDDING.

Put in a pan half a pound of flour, ditto bread crumbs finely grated, three-quarters of a pound of chopped beef suet, a pound of raisins picked and stoned, ditto currants, a few sweet almonds chopped, and half a pound of cut candied peel. Then put in a basin some sugar according to taste, a little mixed spice, a little salt, and a good grate of ginger; add the gratings of two lemons and the juice of one; also a wineglass of brandy and two of raisin wine; beat eight eggs, and add them to the sugar, spices, lemon peel and juice, and wine; then make a hole in the pudding, and pour in the mixture; stir well together for half an hour; butter your mould, and pour in the pudding; tie up the mould in a cloth, and boil six hours.

RAVENSWORTH PUDDING.

Bake three large apples, and then pulp them; take one pint

of cream, two handfuls of fine bread crumbs, a half a pound of pounded loaf sugar, the grated rind of two lemons, and six eggs, using only the yolks of four; mix all together well, beating the eggs thoroughly, the yolks first, then the whites. Well butter a pudding-mould, throw in a handful of fine bread crumbs, toss them well, so that they may stick to the butter all around the mould, and shake out any that are loose; then pour in the above mixture, and bake an hour and a half. Serve immediately with wine sauce.

MANCHESTER PUDDING.

Flavor half a pint of milk with a little lemon peel by infusing it for half an hour; strain it on three ounces of grated bread, and boil it for two or three minutes; add four eggs, leaving the whites of two, two ounces of butter, three tablespoonfuls of brandy, and sugar to taste; stir all these ingredients well together; line a pie-dish with puff-paste, and at the bottom put a thick layer of jam; pour the above mixture cold on the jam, and bake for an hour. Serve cold, with sifted sugar sprinkled over.

KISSES.

Beat the whites of four eggs to a stiff froth; add the juice of a lemon or a little rose-water. Roll and sift half a pound of the whitest loaf sugar, and beat it with the egg. Spread out white paper on buttered tins, and drop a tablespoonful of this mixture on the paper. The oven should be moderately hot, and when the tops have become hard, remove them. Have solution of gum arabic, and dip the lower side of the cake, and join it to another.

CREAM CUSTARD FOR DESSERT ICES.

Take a quart of fresh cream, and whisk four eggs; put them with the cream, with eight ounces powdered loaf sugar, place the whole upon a stove, and stir the mixture with a whisk constantly, taking care it does not "boil," or it will turn to curds. When the custard becomes of a thick consistence, immediately take it from the fire, and strain it through a hair sieve. This can now be flavored with vanilla, &c.

DRYING HERBS.

Herbs should be gathered as soon as they begin to open their flowers. In drying them, two methods are employed. One is to tie them in bunches as soon as cut, and hang them up in a room or shed; the other is to first lay them out in the sun to dry. By both these methods the quality is deteriorated. If fermentation takes place sufficient to discolor the leaves—such as occurs, more or less, when herbs are tied up in bunches whilst green and sappy—their best properties are destroyed. In drying herbs, an open shed or room, where plenty of air can be given, is necessary. Stretch out a piece of netting, such as is used for protecting fruit from birds—wire netting, if at hand, will do; on this lay the herbs, (which should be cut when quite dry,) thinly. Thus treated, air acts upon them from all sides, and they dry quickly, which is the primary object, without losing their best properties. When perfectly dry, put them loosely in white paper bags, tie them up, and hang them where they will be free from damp, or they will become mouldy. Herbs treated in this way will be found but little inferior to such as are fresh cut.

BAKED HADDOCK.

Clean and dry the haddock, make a stuffing of bread crumbs, a bit of suet chopped, or a little very nice dripping, the yolk of an egg, minced parsley, thyme and winter savory, pepper and salt, and a little grated lemon peel. Stuff the fish with this stuffing, put them into a baking-dish, with butter or dripping over them, and about a pint of broth or water, and bake them in a moderate oven. Baste the fish several times while cooking, and flour it well, which will thicken the gravy. Bake from one hour to an hour and a half.

BAKED APPLE AND ALMOND PUDDING.

A quarter of a pound of sweet almonds and a quarter of a pound of loaf sugar; pound all well together, then add the well-beaten yolks of six eggs. Grate the peel of one lemon, add the juice of it, and one tablespoonful of flour. Mix well all together; whip the whites of the six eggs to a stiff froth, and mix them with the other ingredients before baking. Pour the whole upon a thick layer of stewed apples, already prepared in a baking-tin, and bake in a moderate oven until brown.

HOT CRAB.

Carefully pick out the inside of the crab and the large claws and mince them, mixing them thoroughly and seasoning with cayenne pepper and salt. Rub up a teaspoonful or rather less of good curry powder in a little cold gravy or cream, or equal proportions of both, and mix these with the crab, adding a teaspoonful of Chili vinegar and some finely-grated bread crumbs; clean out the shell very carefully, and place the mixture in it, sifting bread crumbs over, add a little butter, and then brown it well with a salamander.

BAKED HALIBUT, CREOLE STYLE.

Put a halibut steak weighing about a pound in the middle of a pan; sprinkle it with salt and a little onion chopped fine; then spread with tomato enough to cover the fish; next cover with bread crumbs. Add a little butter and salt, then garnish the dish with more tomatoes, and bake twenty minutes.

MUTTON COLLOPS.

Cut some very thin slices from a cold leg or the chump end of a loin of mutton, sprinkle them with pepper, salt, pounded mace, minced savory herbs, and minced shalot. Fry them in butter, stir in a dessertspoonful of flour, add half a pint of gravy and one tablespoonful of lemon juice, simmer very gently for about five or seven minutes, and serve immediately

STEWED SWEETBREADS.

Trim some sweetbreads and soak them in warm water till quite white, blanch in boiling water, and then put them in cold water for a short time. When cold dry them, and put them in some well-flavored white stock; stew for half an hour; beat up the yolks of two or three eggs with some cream, a little finely-minced parsley and grated nutmeg, pepper and salt to taste. Add this to the sauce, put it on the fire to get quite hot, dish the sweetbreads, pour the sauce over, and serve.

THE WASSAIL-BOWL.

By those who can afford it, the wassail-bowl should be composed of sherry, well spiced and sweetened, reeking hot, flavored with lemon, and with roasted apples floating on the surface. Ale may be substituted for wine for those of inferior resources. "It is a good-natured bowl, and accommodates itself to the means of all classes, rich and poor; you may have it of the costliest wine or the humblest malt liquor. But in no case must the roasted apples be forgotten." The lamb's wool of our ancestors was nothing else but the wassail which we are describing. You may stir up the compound with a sprig of rosemary, if you wish to be baronial in the enjoyment of the admirable beverage.

MACEDOINE JELLY.

Ingredients: Two ounces Nelson's opaque gelatine, five lemons, eight ounces white sugar, one pint and a half of water, the whites of three eggs, and some fresh fruit. Soak the gelatine in the water for one hour, then add the juice of the lemons, the sugar, and the whites of eggs whisked in a little cold water; stir all together gently over the fire until boiling, allow it to settle a few minutes, then pass through a flannel jelly-bag, pouring it back a few times until quite clear; procure some fresh fruit, such as a few grapes, a few cherries, strawberries, greengages, and one small apple cut in slices, place them in a jelly mould, and stand the mould in cold water; then pour some of the liquid jelly on the top, allow it to set, then fill the mould with the rest of the jelly; place away to set; when required for the table dip the mould in warm water for a few seconds, and wipe with a cloth and turn on a silver or glass dish before sending to table; place a little fresh fruit round the base of the jelly.

LEMON CHEESECAKE.

Line a small dish with puff-paste a quarter of an inch thick, then place a rim on the border of the dish with puff-paste of the same thickness; trim off the edges with a knife, and press the paste well from the centre of the dish towards the edges; then fill it with the following mixture: Into a stew-pan place one-quarter pound butter, six ounces powdered white sugar, three eggs, the grated rind and the juice of two lemons, mix well together, and stir gently over a clear fire until it boils; take the stew-pan immediately off, and stand in a basin of cold water; when cold fill the cheesecake, and bake it in a warm oven until the crust is baked. Send to table on a napkin.

RICE FLUMMERY.

Put into a stew-pan one quart of milk, six ounces white sugar, one-half ounce isinglass, four ounces ground rice; let these boil gently together half an hour, occasionally stirring; when cooked add a drop of essence of almonds, half a glass of brandy; color half pink with cochineal, the other leave white; place one of the two in the bottom of a jelly mould, and when nearly cold turn in the other; when required for the table turn out in the same manner as directed for the jelly.

FRIARS' CHICKEN.

Quarter two or three chickens, and put them into a sauce-pan with one pint and a half of water; add a few sprigs of parsley, some mace, pepper and salt to taste; simmer very slowly until the meat will separate into flakes. Just before serving, beat up three or four eggs, and stir them, off the fire, into the broth. Serve in a deep dish.

ROMAN PUDDING.

Butter a basin and line it with boiled maccaroni, round like a bee-hive; have ready veal, ham, tongue, chicken or cold game, all cut very finely; one ounce Parmesan cheese, and a little nutmeg, pepper, salt, lemon peel and cayenne, two eggs and a cupful of cream; mix all together and fill your basin. Boil for half an hour, glaze it, and serve with good brown gravy.

MUTTON CUTLETS IN THE PORTUGUESE WAY.

Cut the chops, and half fry them with sliced shalot or onion, chopped parsley, and two bay-leaves; season with pepper and salt; then lay a forcemeat on a piece of white paper, put the chops on it, and twist the paper up, leaving a hole for the end of the bones to go through. Broil on a gentle fire. Serve with sauce Robert, or a little gravy.

ROAST VEAL.

Season a breast of veal with pepper and salt; skewer the sweetbread firmly in its place, flour the meat, and roast it slowly before a moderate fire for about two hours—it should be of a fine brown but not dry; baste it with butter. When done, put the gravy in a stew-pan, add a piece of butter rolled in browned flour, and if there should not be quite enough gravy, add a little more water, with pepper and salt to the taste. The gravy should be brown.

TO KEEP EGGS.

Eggs may be kept good for an indefinite period by the following method: Put them in an open-work basket or colander, and immerse them for a moment in boiling water, letting them stay just long enough to form a film on the inside of the shell, which excludes the air. Then place them in some convenient vessel, small end down, and set them in the coolest part of the cellar, where they will keep till wanted for use.

TO PRESERVE EGGS.

Eggs may be preserved for several months by greasing them all over with melted mutton suet and wedging them close together, with the small end downward, in a box of bran. To keep them for winter use, pour a gallon of boiling water on two quarts of quicklime and half a pound of salt; when cold, mix with it one ounce cream of tartar, and the following day put in the eggs.

BUTTERED EGGS.

Hard boil and chop the eggs; put them in a stew-pan with butter, season with pepper, chopped mushroom and parsley, or chopped onion and gherkin; blend all together with a raw egg, and serve on hot toast.

POOR MAN'S PIE.

Take the remains of cold sole, haddock, whiting or hake. Chop and pound it up with butter, a teaspoonful of French mustard, a little chutnee, a fragment of garlic, and a few drops of Chili vinegar. Put it into a pie-dish, cover it with mashed potato, which must be nicely browned.

TO CURE A HAM.

One ounce of saltpetre, one ounce of black pepper ground, one ounce of juniper berries bruised, one pound of common salt, two pounds of brown sugar; mix all this together, and put on your ham; rub and trim it every day for a month, then hang it up in a chimney where wood is burned.

BLACKBERRY CORDIAL.

Ripest berries; mash, put in a linen bag, squeeze out the juice; one pound of the best loaf sugar to every quart of juice; put in a preserving sauce-pan, and, when melted, set on the fire and boil to a thin jelly; when cold, to every quart of juice allow a quart of brandy; stir well and bottle. Ready for use at once.

CHOCOLATE CAKE.

Two small cups of sugar, half a cup of butter, three eggs, one cup of milk, four ounces of chocolate, three cups of flour, one tablespoonful of vanilla extract, one teaspoonful of soda, two of cream of tartar; mix the cake first, and when it is well beaten, take the chocolate, and stir it in carefully. This makes an excellent cake.

SPRAT TOAST.

Bone as many sprats as you require. This can be easily done if they are plainly fried in salt. Pound them up well with butter, pepper, salt, chopped onion, chopped parsley, and enough Swiss milk to moisten it to a paste; heat it for a few moments, and serve on slices of fried bread or hot buttered toast. Herrings, pilchards, and the remains of any cold fish may be utilized in this way.

STEWED OYSTERS.

Drain the liquor from two quarts of firm, plump oysters, mix with it a small teacupful of hot water and a little salt and pepper, and set over the fire in a sauce-pan. When it boils, add a large cupful of rich milk. Let it boil up once, add the oysters, and let them boil five minutes. When they ruffle, add two tablespoonfuls of butter, and the instant it is melted and well stirred in, take off the fire.

TO STUFF A HAM.

Select a nice ham and boil it; when done, let it get cold before you skin and trim it. Prepare a stuffing of bread crumbs, butter, pepper, parsley, thyme and celery. Begin at the hock, and make incisions with a sharp knife, about an inch apart; put in the stuffing as you draw out the knife. Rub in a bowl the yolks of two hard-boiled eggs, and brandy sufficient to make a paste; spread it on the ham smoothly, and grate over it bread crumbs; stick in cloves; ornament. Put it in the oven, and let it brown gently. Eaten cold.

TO BAKE A HAM.

Unless when too salt from not being sufficiently soaked, a ham (particularly a young and fresh one) eats much better baked than boiled, and remains longer good. The safer plan is to lay it in plenty of cold water over night. The following day soak it for an hour or more in warm water, wash it delicately clean, trim smoothly off all rusty parts, and lay it with the rind downwards in a coarse paste, rolled to about an inch thick; moisten the edges, draw and pinch them together, and fold them over on the upper side of the ham, taking care to close them so that no gravy can escape. Send it to a well-heated but not a fierce oven. A very small ham will require three hours' baking, and a large one five. The crust and the skin must be removed while it is hot. When only part of a ham is dressed, this mode is better far than boiling it.

BAKED MACKEREL.

Wash, scale and empty as many fresh mackerel as required; make a stuffing of mashed potatoes, bread crumbs, sweet herbs, minced onion, pepper, salt and beaten egg; stuff each fish, and replace the roes, if you have any; sew up the slit, and put the mackerel in a well-floured baking-pan, heads and tails together; bake slowly for one hour. Serve hot.

MARION CAKE.

Put together in a pan fourteen ounces of sifted loaf sugar, the yolks of eight eggs, eight ounces of fine white flour, and a tablespoonful of orange-flower water. Beat all together till thoroughly mixed. Whip a pint of cream till light, and whisk the whites of the eight eggs to a thick froth. Beat these into the other ingredients, and put in a pan lined with buttered paper. Bake in a quick oven half an hour.

BAKED RICE PUDDING.

Boil together in a sauce-pan one pint of milk and the grated peel of a small lemon. In another sauce-pan boil a teacupful of rice until tender, and, when done, drain off all the water. Beat four eggs till light, stir them into the milk with an ounce of fresh butter, a quarter of a pound of stoned raisins, a quarter of a pound of sugar, a little grated nutmeg, and two tablespoonfuls of rose-water. Add the rice. Stir all well together, and bake in a buttered tin half an hour.

POTTED MEAT.

Take any well-roasted or boiled meat, remove all gristle, hard pieces and fat from it, mince, and then pound it in a mortar with a little butter, reduced gravy, and a spoonful of Worcestershire sauce; beat it to a smooth paste, seasoning during the process with pounded cloves and allspice, mace or grated nutmeg, salt and a little cayenne. Put the mixture into pots, press it close down, cover with clarified butter, and keep it in a cool, dry place.

TO CURE TONGUES.

For a tongue that weighs seven pounds, put one ounce of saltpetre, half an ounce of black pepper, two ounces of sugar, and three ounces of juniper berries. In two days it will be fit for cooking. Take care to have the gullet cut away before it is cooked.

HAM TOAST.

Scrape or pound some cold ham, mix it with beaten egg, season with pepper, lay it upon buttered toast, and place it in a hot oven for three or four minutes. Dried salmon, smoked tongue, potted meats, or any other relishing viands, answer equally well upon toast.

FINE PANCAKES.

Take a pint of cream, eight eggs, (leave out two of the whites,) three large spoonfuls of orange-flower water, a little sugar and grated nutmeg; melt a small quantity of butter with the cream over the fire, then add three spoonfuls of flour, and mix well together; butter the frying-pan for the first; let them run as thin as you can in the pan, fry them quick, and send them up hot.

FOWL AND RICE CROQUETTES.

Put half pound rice into one quart of stock, and let it boil very gently for half an hour, then add three ounces butter, and simmer it till quite dry and soft; when cold, make it into balls, hollow out the inside, and fill with minced fowl made rather thick, cover over with rice, dip the balls into egg, sprinkle them with bread-crumbs, and fry a nice brown; dish them, and garnish with fried parsley, oysters, white sauce. or a little cream may be stirred into the rice before it cools.

POTATO CHIPS.

Peel a raw potato as apples are peeled; let the parings be as near as possible the same thickness, and let them be as long as possible; dry them thoroughly in a cloth, put them in the frying-basket, and plunge it in boiling hot lard; when the chips are a golden color, drain them well in front of the fire, sprinkle fine salt over them, and serve with roast game.

EGG WINE.

Beat an egg, and mix with it a tablespoonful of cold water; make half a glass of cold water and one glass of sherry hot, but not boiling, pour it upon the egg, stirring all the time, add a little lump sugar and grated nutmeg; put all into a very clean saucepan, set it on a gentle fire, and stir the contents one way, until they thicken, but they must not boil; serve in a glass with sippets of toasted bread or plain crisp biscuits. If the egg is not warmed, the mixture will be found easier of digestion, but it is not so pleasant a drink.

VEGETABLE MARROW PRESERVE.

Peel the marrow, take out the seeds and cut in strips like marmalade; put a pound of loaf sugar to each pound of strips, letting it lie all night to draw juice; next day put rind grated and juice of one large lemon to each pound of the mixture; boil all till clear, which will take quite an hour.

FRENCH RICE PUDDING.

Boil a cupful of rice in milk until it is well swollen; add three eggs well beaten, a quarter of a pound of raisins of the sun, (as these do not require stoning,) a little sugar and nutmeg, all beaten up together with the rice; fill a mou'., and bake for three-quarters of an hour.

APPLE CREAM.

Make a good custard pretty thick, put it in a glass dish; take three or four baked apples, rub the pulp through a sieve; add four ounces of sugar sifted to the pulp, the whites of two new-laid eggs, the juice of half a lemon whipped for a full hour; then put it in spoonfuls on the apple as lightly as you can.

LEMON CREAM.

Boil the rind of a lemon pared very thin in half a pint of water till yellow, then strain it off and let it stand till cold; add the juice of two lemons, the yolks of two eggs and the whites of three; sugar to your taste; stir all together on a slow fire till as thick as cream; pour it into jelly glasses when cold.

CABINET PUDDING.

Split and stone three dozen fine raisins, or take an equal number of dried cherries, and place them regularly in a sort of pattern in a thickly-buttered plain quart mould or basin; next slice and lay into it three penny sponge-cakes; add to these two ounces ratafias, four maccaroons, an ounce and a half candied citron sliced thin, the yolks of four eggs (with whites of three only) thoroughly whisked, mixed with half pint new milk, then strained, to half pint sweet cream, and sweetened with two ounces and a half pounded sugar; these ought to fill the mould exactly. Steam the pudding, or boil it very gently for one hour. Let it stand a few minutes before dished, and serve with good sauce.

GALETTE.

This cake is a great favorite in France. Sift a pound of the best flour, put it in a heap on the pastry-board, make a hole in the middle, put into it a pinch of salt and one of sifted sugar, three-quarters of a pound of butter, and a gill of water. Knead the ingredients together, and when they begin to mix, sprinkle over by degrees half a gill of water, continuing to knead with the palm of the hand, and, when the paste is perfectly smooth, make it into a ball, and let it lie for an hour. At the end of this time, roll out the paste to the thickness of half an inch; mark the edges as for Scotch shortbread, put the cake on a baking-sheet, brush over the top with yolk of egg, and score it in the form of diamonds. Bake in a quick oven for half an hour, or until the galette is elastic on the pressure of the finger.

IRISH STEW.

Take part of a neck of mutton, cut it into small pieces, put it into a kettle, the meat well covered with water; some onions cut in slices, pepper and salt; a number of potatoes must be cut rather larger than the meat (not sliced); put them at the top, let all stew together till done. A breast is nice done this way.

APPLE PUDDING.

Take three large baking apples, pare them, and cut the cores square out, and fill the holes with butter and sugar, and a little of any seasoning preferred. Butter a deep dish, lay the apples in it, and cover them with batter, such as the fritters are made of, and bake in a quick oven about half an hour.

PEACH PIE.

Take mellow, juicy peaches, wash and put them in a deep pie-dish lined with pie-crust, sprinkle a thick layer of sugar on each layer of peaches, put in about a tablespoonful of water, and sprinkle a little flour over the top; cover it with a thick crust, and bake the pie from fifty to sixty minutes.

BROILED SALMON.

Slices from a fresh salmon, well scaled, cleansed and wiped; two ounces of butter, melted; one teaspoonful of flour; one saltspoonful of salt; melt the butter smoothly, thicken it with flour, add the salt, and roll the salmon well in it; make a very clear fire, take a perfectly clean gridiron, and broil carefully; time, ten minutes.

CUSTARDS WITHOUT EGGS.

One quart of new milk, four tablespoonfuls of flour, two of sugar; season with nutmeg or cinnamon, and add salt to your liking. The milk should be placed over a quick fire, and, when at a boiling point, the flour should be added, being previously stirred up in cold milk. As soon as thoroughly scalded, add the sugar, spices and salt. This is an excellent dish, and deservedly prized by every one who has tried it.

PICKLED CUCUMBERS.

To pickle cucumbers to keep through the winter, steep in strong brine for a week, then pour it off, heat it to boiling, and pour it over the cucumbers. In twenty-four hours drain on a cloth, pack in wide-mouthed bottles, fill these with strong hot pickling vinegar, and seal at once. Various spices may be added in the bottles.

PARMESAN OMELET.

Beat up three eggs, with pepper and salt to taste, and a tablespoonful of grated Parmesan cheese; put a piece of butter, the size of an egg, into the omelet-pan; as soon as it is melted, pour in the eggs, and, holding the handle of the pan with one hand, stir the omelet with the other by means of a flat spoon. The moment the omelet begins to set, cease stirring, but keep shaking the pan for a minute or so; then, with the spoon, double up the omelet, and keep on shaking the pan until the under side is of a good color; turn it out on a hot dish, colored side uppermost, and serve.

PICKLED BEANS.

Put into two gallons of water enough salt to float an egg; then boil the salt and water for ten minutes, and put it away to get cold. Pick French beans or scarlet runners before they are stringy, put them whole into an earthenware crock, and pour the above pickle over them. Have ready a piece of wood that will entirely cover them; lay a cloth over the beans, and then put on the piece of wood and a heavy weight to press them under the pickle. Not more than twenty pounds of beans should be kept in one crock, as they do not keep well in large quantities. They keep crisp and good for seven months, if in a dry place. About once a fortnight the cloth should be rinsed in boiling water and then in cold, as a scum will often rise. When required for use, take out a sufficient quantity, soak them for six hours, changing the water once or twice; then cut them up for table, and boil them like fresh beans. They are very acceptable when vegetables are limited in quantity and poor in quality.

GERMAN YEAST.

This is only the ordinary beer yeast, kept fresh and fit for use for several months, by placing it in a close canvas bag, and gently and gradually squeezing out the moisture in a screw-press, until the remaining matter acquires the consistency of clay or soft cheese, in which state it must be preserved in close vessels, or wrapped in waxen cloth.

POUND CAKE.

1. Take one pound each of sugar, butter, eggs, and flour, mixed into a paste, with a teacupful of milk, half an ounce of sal volatile being added to make them light. 2. Take one and a quarter pounds of butter, the same of loaf sugar, one pint of eggs, three-quarters of an ounce of volatile salt, a teacupful of milk, and three pounds of flour. 3. Take one pint of eggs, one pound of loaf sugar, six ounces of butter, two pounds of flour, half an ounce of volatile salt. Beat the butter to a cream in a smooth-glazed warm earthenware dish, stir in the sugar by degrees, then the eggs; also, gradually, before they are all in, add a part of the flour, and mix it with the remaining portion of the eggs well together; then dissolve the volatile salt in the milk; add a little of this and of the flour alternately, till the whole have been added, and until all the ingredients are well incorporated together. It may now be poured into buttered tins, surrounded by paper, filling them about three parts full, and sprinkling a few currants at the top of each. The whole mixing should be completed as rapidly as possible, and the cakes immediately put into a slow oven. To know when it is done, thrust a small wooden skewer into it; if dry when taken out, the cake is done; if sticky, it must be baked longer. 4. Beat one pound of butter in an earthen pan until it is like a fine thick cream, then beat in nine whole eggs till quite light; put in a glass of brandy, a little lemon-peel shred fine, then work in one and a quarter pounds of flour; put it into a hoop or pan and bake it for an hour. A pound plum cake is made the same, with putting one and a half pounds of cleaned washed currants and half a pound of candied lemon-peel.

POTATO JELLY.

To obtain this jelly in perfection, let a potato be washed, peeled, and grated; throw the pulp, thus procured, into a jug of water, and stir it well. Pass the mixture of pulp and water over a sieve, and collect the water which passes through into a basin. Let this stand for a few minutes, and sufficient quantity of starch will have fallen for the purpose required. Pour off the water, and then keep stirring up the starch at the bottom of the basin, while boiling water is being poured upon it, and it will soon and suddenly pass to the state of a jelly. The only nicety required is to be careful that the water is absolutely boiling, otherwise the change will not take place. It does not require more than eight minutes to change a raw potato into a basinful of most excellent jelly, which has only to be seasoned with a little sugar, nutmeg and white wine, to please the most fastidious palate.

RAISINS.

To stone raisins easily, pour boiling water over them and drain it off; this loosens the stones, and they come out clean and with ease.

ANGELS ON HORSEBACK.

Place a large cooking oyster in a piece of fat bacon, tie it up with cotton, and just toast it for a moment before the fire. Serve on a piece of toast.

POUNDED POTATOES—IRISH WAY.

Peel a sufficient quantity of potatoes while raw, after having been well washed; pick out all discolored bits, eyes, etc.; put them into cold water; when boiled—that is, when they break on a fork being stuck into them—drain them, scatter a handful of salt over them, cover with a clean dry cloth, and let the saucepan stand on the range or hob until they are well steamed; take off the saucepan, set it on the floor, and with a wooden instrument, called in Ireland a "beetle," pound them well; add a good lump of butter—a couple of ounces—and about half a pint of sweet milk, added by degrees; pound until the potatoes are quite smooth; then set the saucepan back on the range to reheat thoroughly before dishing.

TAPIOCA JELLY.

Take four tablespoonfuls of tapioca, rinse it thoroughly, then soak it five hours, in cold water enough to cover it. Set a pint of cold water on the fire; when it boils, mash and stir up the tapioca that is in the water and mix it with the boiling water; let the whole simmer gently, with a stick of cinnamon or mace. When thick and clear, mix a couple of tablespoonfuls of white sugar, with half a tablespoonful of lemon-juice and half a glass of white wine; stir it into the jelly. If not sweet enough, add more sugar, and turn the jelly into cups.

GINGERBREAD NUTS.

Take one pound flour, half a pound treacle, half a pound sugar, a quarter pound butter, half ounce ground ginger, sixteen drops essence of lemon, potash the size of a nut, dissolved in a tablespoonful of hot water; mix all together. Butter a baking-tin, and drop the mixture on it in lumps the size of a walnut, a good distance apart. Bake in a moderate oven. Keep in tins closely covered.

VEAL BROTH.

Stew a knuckle of veal of four or five pounds in three quarts of water, with two blades of mace, an onion, a head of celery, and a little parsley, pepper and salt; let the whole simmer very gently until the liquor is reduced to two quarts; then take out the meat, when the mucilaginous parts are done, and serve up with parsley and butter. Add to the broth either two ounces rice, separately boiled, or of vermaceli; put in only long enough to be stewed tender. Dish the knuckle separately, and serve it with parsley and butter.

TO PRESERVE BUTTER.

Melt it in an earthen vessel, surrounded with warm water; skim the butter until clear, and pour the pure portion off into pots, which should be filled to the top and closely covered. A little salt may be added before pouring, and should be stirred in, afterwards allowing the butter to clear. Or, mix two ounces of salt with one ounce each of saltpetre and white sugar; add one ounce of this mixture, in fine powder, to each pound of butter, working it well in. The butter must not be used for a month, and the pots containing it must be filled to the brim.

NORWICH BISCUITS.

Take six pounds of flour, eight or ten ounces of butter, and one quart of milk. A little sugar may be added, but it is not usually employed. Warm half of the milk to a blood heat, then add yeast enough to make it slightly bitter, rub into this about one pound of the flour, and put it in a warm place. It will soon rise, and after a little time fall again. Now rub the butter into the flour with the remaining portion of the milk warmed as before. Add it all to the sponge, and set it in a warm place to rise a second time. Separate portions of this dough, which should be rather stiff, making eighteen or twenty pieces from a pound of dough; mould them into a round ball under your hands, place them on slightly-buttered tins, from two to three inches asunder, flatten them a little, and stamp them with a docker. Prove them, and bake in rather a cool oven, so as to admit of their being baked through, that they may eat short and crisp; if they should not be sufficiently dried when taken out, finish them in the stove. At Norwich they are baked on the bottom of the oven. These biscuits are commonly called in London milk biscuits, and are recommended as children's food, being supposed to be made without butter. Also they go by different names in some parts of the country, as fingers, half-moons, fancy biscuits, and tea biscuits, and are made of various forms.

MIXED PICKLE.

To each gallon of vinegar allow one-quarter pound bruised ginger, one-quarter pound mustard, one-quarter pound salt, two ounces mustard seed, one and a-half ounces turmeric, one ounce ground black pepper, one-quarter ounce cayenne; cauliflowers, onions, celery, sliced cucumbers. Have a large jar with a tightly-fitting lid, in which put as much vinegar as is required, reserving a little to mix the various powders to a smooth paste. Put into a basin the mustard, turmeric, pepper, and cayenne; mix them with vinegar, and stir until no lumps remain; add all the ingredients to the vinegar and mix well. Keep this liquor in a warm place and stir thoroughly every morning with a wooden spoon for near a month, when it will be ready for the vegetables to be added. As these come into season have them gathered on a dry day, and after merely wiping them with a cloth to free them from moisture, put them into the pickle. The cauliflowers should be divided into small bunches. Put all the vegetables into the pickle raw, and at the end of the season, when the vegetables are all procured, store away in jars and tie over with a bladder. As none of the ingredients are boiled, this pickle will not be fit for eating for several months. The contents must be stirred each morning.

WILD DUCK.

Wild duck, if fishy, and the flavor is disliked, should be scalded for a few minutes in salt and water before roasting. If the flavor is very strong, the duck may be skinned, as the oil of the skin is the objectionable part. After skinning, spread with butter and thickly dredge with flour before putting in a very quick oven.

SCOTCH CREAM.

Put skim milk over night in a tub which has a plug at the bottom, and put this tub into another filled with hot water. In the morning take out the small tub and draw off the thin part of the milk, until the thick sour cream begins to come. This process requires practice as to the heat of the water; when it succeeds, skimmed milk yields nearly half of this cream, which is eaten with sugar as a delicacy. It is only distinguishable from cream by its taste.

SHORT BREAD.

Take one and a-quarter pounds of flour, half a pound of sugar, half a pound of butter, three eggs, quarter of an ounce of volatile salts, and a little essence of lemon. Make four cakes out of five ounces of dough, mould into a round form, then roll them out into an oval shape, pinch them around the edges, put a piece of candied lemon peel at the top, and bake slowly.

CELERY WITH WHITE SAUCE.

Trim the roots and cut to about six inches three heads of celery, wash them carefully, tie them together with string; put them in a saucepan with an onion, a blade of mace, some whole pepper, salt, and sufficient boiling water to cover them. Let them boil till quite done, then drain them, remove the string, and serve with the following sauce over them: Melt one ounce butter in a saucepan, and mix with it a dessertspoonful of flour, add as much of the water in which the celery was boiled as is wanted to make the sauce, put salt to taste, and stir in off the fire the yolk of an egg, beaten up with the juice of a lemon and strained.

TO BOIL CODFISH.

Crimped cod is preferable to the plain, it is likewise better cut in slices than cooked whole; to boil it well have the water ready boiling, with one pound of salt to every six quarts; put in the fish, draw the fish-kettle to the corner of the fire, where let it simmer slowly from twenty minutes to half an hour; when done, the bone in the centre will draw out easily; if boiled too much it will eat tough and stringy. Should the fish not be crimped, add more salt to the water; it will cause the fish to eat firmer. Oyster sauce and plain melted butter are served with codfish.

BATH BUNS.

Take one pound of flour, to one-third of it add in a hole in the centre a tablespoonful of yeast and a teacupful of warm milk, let it stand for an hour in a warm place to rise. When risen, add six ounces butter and four eggs, with the rest of the flour, six ounces sugar and a little pounded cinnamon to taste; mix all well together, cover it over, and let it rise again. Shape it into buns, leaving it as rough as possible, sift some sugar and a few comfits on the top, sprinkle with a little water, and bake in a moderate oven on well-buttered tins.

NOYEAU.

1. Take one and a-half gallons of French brandy, six ounces of the best French prunes, two ounces of celery, three ounces of the kernels of apricots, nectarines, and peaches, one ounce of bitter almonds, all gently bruised, essence of orange peel and essence of lemon peel, each, two pennyweights; and half a pound of loaf sugar. Let the whole stand ten days or a fortnight, then draw off, and add to the clear noyeau as much rose water as will make it up to two gallons. 2. Blanched bitter almonds, one ounce; proof spirit, one quart; lump sugar, one pound; dissolved in half a pint of water; digest and filter. 3. Bitter almonds, blanched, three ounces; coriander seed, quarter of an ounce; cinnamon, ginger, and mace, of each, one drachm; proof spirit, two quarts; white sugar, two pounds; dissolved in one and a-half pints of water. Macerate for a week, and fine down with quarter of an ounce of alum. 4. To one gallon spirits of wine or white brandy add two drachms of the oil of Seville oranges, four pounds of apricot and peach kernels. Beat them up in a mortar before you mix them with the brandy, then put them into it, and shake them up two or three times a day for three days; add the oil, killed, and one quart of cherry-juice. 5. Instead of the kernels, put for the above quantity, half an ounce of the oil of bitter almonds; sweeten and color to fancy. Noyeau must never be drank except in small quantities, on account of the poisonous character of the oil of the kernels, and from which ingredient it takes its flavor and name.

COD'S ROE FRIED IN BATTER.

Wash the roe well; then put it into a saucepan on the fire, well covered with salted water, to which has been added a little lemon-juice or vinegar. Boil for ten minutes; drain, and leave it to get cold; then cut the roe into slices a quarter of an inch thick, dip the slices of roe into batter, and fry in butter until of a light brown color. Serve, garnished with fried parsley and with slices of lemon. Batter: Beat up together the yolks of two eggs, one tablespoonful of olive oil, and four or five tablespoonfuls of cold water; amalgamate with this three tablespoonfuls of fine flour, and a good pinch of salt; beat the mixture five or ten minutes, adding a little more water, if too thick. Just before using it, stir into it lightly and quickly, the whites of two eggs whisked to a froth.

FRENCH BEANS.

Cut the ends off the beans, string them, and cut them in pieces about one inch long, and put them in cold water with a little salt in it; put in a saucepan two quarts of water, a heaping tablespoonful of salt, a teaspoonful of powdered sugar; let it boil, and, when boiling, throw in the beans; let them boil hard till they sink in the water; drain through a colander, and put in a hot dish; season with butter, pepper and salt.

BAKED OR STEWED CALF'S FOOT.

Well clean one calf's foot, and either stew or bake it for three to four hours in one pint of milk, one pint of water, one blade of mace, the rind of half a lemon, pepper and salt to taste. An onion and a small quantity of celery may be added, if approved. Half a teacupful of cream stirred in, just before it is taken, is a great improvement.

FRICASSEE OF FOWL.

Cut a fowl or chicken into eight pieces: that is, the two wings and legs, dividing the back and breast into two pieces each; wash well, put them into a stewpan and cover with water, season with a teaspoonful of salt, a little pepper, a bunch of parsley, four cloves, and a blade of mace; let boil twenty minutes, pass the stock through a sieve into a basin, take out the pieces of fowl, trim well; then, in another stewpan, put two ounces butter, with which mix a good spoonful of flour, moisten with the stock, and put in the pieces of fowl; stir occasionally until boiling, skim, add twenty button onions, let simmer until the onions are tender, when add a gill of cream, with which you have mixed the yolks of two eggs; stir it quickly over the fire, but do not let it boil; take out the pieces, dress upon your dish, sauce over, and serve.

BAKED CALF'S HEAD.

Boil the head until you can pick out all the bones, and keep the water the head is boiled in; take your pieces and lay them in a dish, having cut them small; use some salt, pepper, a little parsley, a grate of nutmeg, a small piece of butter and some dry breadcrumbs, say a teacupful of the latter; moisten it all with some of the water the head has been boiled in; put in a baking-dish, and let it bake half an hour; take the yolks of two eggs, and make a sauce with the boiled liquor; make soup of the rest of the liquor.

BEEFSTEAK STEWED WITHOUT WATER.

Get three pounds or four pounds rumpsteak, cut about an inch thick; put one ounce of butter in a frying-pan large enough to hold your steak, and let the butter melt without browning; wash the steak quickly in cold water, and put it in the frying-pan, covering closely. As soon as it is thoroughly heated, season with a teaspoonful of salt and a saltspoonful of white pepper; then push the pan back on the stove where it will simmer—not boil—keeping it covered all the time, and a weight on the cover. It will be found to be cooked and perfectly tender in an hour and a half Put on a hot dish, and add half a teacupful of tomato or two tablespoonfuls of walnut catsup to the gravy in the pan, and pour it over the steak.

BAKED BEEF TEA.

Cut one pound fleshy beef into small pieces; take away all the fat, and put into a baking-jar with half a pint of water and half a saltspoonful of salt. Cover the jar well, and place it in a warm but not hot oven, and bake for three or four hours; it should be strained, and kept in a cool place until wanted. It may also be flavored with an onion, a clove, and some sweet herbs if the invalid is strong enough to take them.

MINCED CHICKEN OR MUTTON WITH EGGS, FOR INVALIDS.

Take, if chicken, some of the white meat from the breast, and remove all skin and outside parts; if mutton, an underdone slice or two from the leg, saddle, or loin; mince it very finely; put it into a stewpan with a little very good strong gravy or beef tea, free from fat; flavor it, if liked, with a few herbs and spices, and simmer gently until quite hot, but not boiling; then thicken it with a little butter and flour, and season to taste with pepper and salt. Put this mince on a small dish, and serve on the top of a nicely-poached egg.

PLAIN CAKE.

To two pounds of flour add half a pound of beef-dripping or bacon-fat, half a pound of sultanas, four ounces of moist sugar, one ounce of lemon-peel, a little salt. Let the flour be dried, then rub into it the dripping, taking care that both are well mixed and free from lumps; shred the lemon-peel finely, and add with the salt, sugar and sultanas, these latter being thoroughly freed from the stalks and gritty matter. Rub all together; make a hole in the centre of the mass, and pour in a tablespoonful of fresh brewers' yeast; then, with warm water, mix the whole well till it is of the consistence of moist dough; well cover, and stand in a warm place to rise, then bake in tins. This quantity will make two large cakes, each of which will take an hour and a half to bake in a moderate oven. If yeast is not procurable, a tablespoonful of Borwick's baking-powder may be substituted; then the cake may be at once put into the tins and consigned to the oven.

COLLEGE PUDDING.

Take eight ounces breadcrumbs, eight ounces suet, eight ounces currants, one ounce citron-peel, one ounce orange-peel, a little sugar and nutmeg, three eggs beaten, yolks and whites separately, and a glass of brandy. Mix well, and shape them into balls; rub them over with egg and roll them in flour. Fry a nice brown in boiling butter or lard, and drain them on blotting-paper; or, they may be put into small molds and baked in the oven. In either case, serve with wine or brandy sauce.

SAVORY RICE.

Chop an onion very fine, and fry it in butter till it be of a gold color; then stir in a teacupful of rice; let it cook in the butter for a few minutes, stirring all the time; then add one pint of good gravy, and let it simmer slowly. When nearly cooked, put a little grated nutmeg, Parmesan cheese, salt and pepper, to taste. Mix it up well, and, when thoroughly done, let it stand a few minutes before the fire, and, just before serving, stir in a small piece more of butter. Serve garnished with croquettes of any kind of meat, with stewed tomatoes—tinned—or with slices of fried bacon.

MUTTON MINCED.

Take some slices of cold mutton, about one-quarter of a pound, free them entirely from fat, gristle and outside parts, and mince them very finely; melt a small piece of butter in a saucepan, and stir into it a tablespoonful of flour; keep stirring till it gets brown, then add half a pint of good stock, some powdered sweet herbs, pepper and salt to taste, and the minced meat; keep on stirring till the mixture is quite hot, add a little chopped parsley, then work into the mixture the yolks of one or two eggs beaten up with a little lemon-juice. Serve within a wall of mashed potatoes, or rice plainly boiled or dressed with tomato sauce.

RICE.

Boil the rice fifteen minutes in salted water; then turn off the water, and pour in a little milk; let it simmer gently till the rice is soft; then let it stand where it will not burn for ten minutes, in order to evaporate the milk, so that the particles of rice may be dry and separate from each other. May be eaten with fruit sauce, or a little sugar or syrup, or as it is.

SLICED POTATOES.

Boil eight large potatoes in their skins, and let them cool. When cold, peel them and cut them into thick slices; put into a stewpan two ounces of butter in a thin slice, and when it is melted, add a teacupful of well-seasoned stock or gravy, a teaspoonful of finely-chopped parsley and a teaspoonful of mixed pepper and salt. Stir these well together over the fire till hot, add the potatoes, simmer five minutes, stir in the juice of a lemon, and serve hot.

POTATO RIBBONS.

Cut the potatoes into slices rather less than an inch thick, free them from the skins, and pare round and round in very long and thin ribbons; place them in a pan of cold water, and, a short time before they are wanted on the table, drain them from the water. Fry them in hot lard or good dripping until they are quite crisp and browned; drain and dry them on a soft cloth, pile them on a hot dish, and season them with salt and cayenne in fine powder.

POTATO PIE.

Have ready a rich crust, lay in the pie-dish slices of boiled sweet potato and thin slices of a mellow apple, then spread thickly sugar and butter; cover with a crust, and bake nicely.

CHICKEN AND HAM PIE.

Season some slices of boiled ham, lay them on a puff-paste about half an inch thick; then season some pieces of chicken and place them on the ham, with the yolks of some hard eggs; cover these with more slices of ham, season as before, put some gravy in, and put a puff-crust on the top, and bake it thoroughly. If to be eaten hot, more gravy may be added when done.

CONSOMÉ À LA REGENCE.

Ingredients: Four pounds lean beef, three onions, three carrots, one turnip, a small bunch of sweet herbs, a sprig of parsley, some seasoning, a little soy, a bunch of watercresses, the whites of five eggs, and four quarts of water. Cut the onions, carrots and turnip into thin slices and lay them in the bottom of a stewpan; cut the beef into small pieces and lay on the top of the vegetables; place on the stove, and allow to cook gently one hour; then add four quarts of water; let it come to the boil, take off the scum as it rises; when entirely free from scum, add a little soy, a bunch of sweet herbs, and a little parsley, some seasoning, and let simmer gently three hours. Lightly butter a tin mould, put in it the whites of five eggs, cover the mould with paper, and place in a stewpan with a little boiling water; cook until the whites are quite firm ; when cooked, cut the whites into small squares ; keep warm until wanted. Throw the leaves of a bunch of watercresses into boiling water to blanch for one minute, then drain on a cloth; strain the soup through a fine cloth, take off any fat that remains, with a sheet of white paper laid lightly on the top; allow it to boil, pour in the tureen, throw in the whites of eggs and the blanched watercresses; serve immediately.

WHITE SOUP À LA BEATRICE.

Ingredients: One fowl, one pound veal, one onion, a little celery, one carrot, some seasoning, three quarts of water, one quart of milk, one gill of cream, two blades of mace, four ounces of lean ham, one tin of preserved green peas, and a little roux. Cut the fowl and veal into pieces, place them in a stewpan with the vegetables cut into slices, add some seasoning, two blades of mace, and three quarts of water ; let boil, take off the scum, and let simmer four hours; strain off the gravy from the fowl and veal, add to it one quart of milk, a gill of cream, and a little roux ; let boil to the consistency of cream, strain through a fine hair sieve. Place in the tureen one tin of preserved green peas previously made hot, and four ounces of lean ham cut into small diamonds; pour the boiling soup over and serve.

SALMON CUTLETS, SWISS SAUCE.

Ingredients: Two pounds of small salmon, a little anchovy sauce, five eggs, some breadcrumbs, seasoning, one pint of stock, two ounces of French capers, and a few preserved mushrooms, a little roux, and lard for frying. Slit the salmon down the middle with a sharp knife, take out the bone and trim off the skin, and cut into slices one-third of an inch thick ; whisk up two eggs, add a little anchovy sauce and some seasoning. Well flour the cutlets, dip them in the egg-mixture, then in the bread crumbs. Ten minutes before dinner-time, have ready some boiling lard and place in the cutlets, (a few at a time,) and fry a golden brown; when cooked, drain on some paper to absorb the fat. Place in a stewpan one pint of good stock, a tablespoonful of anchovy sauce, two ounces capers, and a few mushrooms chopped fine, a little pepper, and some roux; let boil ten minutes, then whisk in three eggs, and let come to the boil. Dish the cutlets on a napkin and garnish with parsley, and serve the sauce in a tureen.

SOLES À LA BONNE FEMME.

Ingredients: Four soles, one onion, a little vinegar, a little parsley, a little thyme, half a pint of stock gravy, some seasoning, and a little roux. Chop one onion and a little parsley very fine, place them in a stewpan with half a pint of stock, some seasoning, a little finely-rubbed thyme, a gill of vinegar, and a little roux, and let boil five minutes. Cut each sole into three pieces, well wash and clean them in lukewarm salt and water, throw them into cold water, wipe each piece dry with a clean cloth, then place them in a stewpan, pour the sauce over them, and let simmer thirty minutes, occasionally turning them with a fishslice. Send to table on a hot dish garnished with croutons of fried bread.

FILLET OF BEEF À LA MOLDAVE.

Ingredients: About five pounds fillet of beef, three onions, three carrots, a few allspice, two bay-leaves, a blade of mace, one quart of stock broth, a small bunch of sweet herbs, four ounces rice, four ounces lean ham, one tin of preserved peas, and some mashed potatoes. Trim the fillet of beef into shape, place the trimmings in a stewpan with three carrots and three onions cut into slices, a few allspice, two bay-leaves, a blade of mace, a small bunch of sweet herbs, some seasoning, and one quart of stock; lay in the beef, cover with buttered paper, place on the lid, let come to the boil on the fire, then place the stewpan in a hot oven for two hours; when cooked, strain off the gravy, take off the fat, and reduce to half a pint by boiling; boil four ounces well-washed rice in boiling water until tender, drain it on a sieve, and keep hot; make hot a tin of preserved peas, and cut four ounces lean ham into small squares; have ready some mashed potatoes; place a bed of mashed potatoes on a hot dish, and place the fillet of beef on the top; put round it alternately, in little heaps, the rice, ham, and peas; pour the boiling gravy over it, and serve very hot.

BOILED CHICKENS, MUSHROOM SAUCE.

Ingredients: Two large or three small chickens, two onions, two blades of mace, one carrot, one bay-leaf, one pint of milk, a tin of preserved mushrooms, some seasoning and a little roux, some slices of lean ham. Place the chickens in boiling water, (enough to cover them,) add a blade of mace and one onion cut in slices, a bay-leaf, and some seasoning; let boil thirty-five minutes; into a stewpan put one pint of milk, a blade of mace, one onion cut in slices, some seasoning, and a little roux; let boil twenty minutes—(if not thick enough, add a little more roux)—strain through a sieve or metal strainer; into the sauce put one tin of preserved mushrooms cut into slices; when cooked, take out the chickens, drain them in a clean cloth, place on a hot dish, and pour the sauce over them; garnish with a few slices of lean ham.

SWEETBREADS AU GRATIN.

Ingredients: Three heart sweetbreads generally suffice for a dish; four ounces butter, one onion, one carrot, a blade of mace. a slice of bacon, a few allspice, one pint of good stock, some seasoning, a little roux, a few breadcrumbs, and some mashed potatoes. Steep the sweetbreads in cold water for one hour, then place them in warm water, and blanch ten minutes; trim them, and press them between two dishes, with a weight on them, until cold; cut up one onion and one carrot into slices, place them in a stewpan with a blade of mace, a slice of bacon, a few allspice, some seasoning, one pint of stock; lay in the sweetbreads, cover with buttered paper, bring to the boil in the stove, then place in the oven to braise for one hour; mash some potatoes, place them on a hot dish, put the sweetbreads on the top, strain the gravy the sweetbreads were braised in, take off the fat, thicken with a little roux, then pour a little of the sauce over the sweetbreads; cover them with breadcrumbs, then pour some more sauce over them, then more breadcrumbs; give them another coating, place a piece of butter on each sweetbread, and then place them in a hot oven for twenty minutes to brown; serve on the same dish.

CALVES' FEET À LA CINTRA.

Ingredients: Three calves' feet, one quart of milk, one onion, one carrot, a bay-leaf, some seasoning, a little roux, four eggs, two lemons, half a pint of lentils, and one quart of stock. Cut the meat off the feet in long strips, place them in a stewpan with one onion and one carrot cut in slices, some seasoning, a bay-leaf, one pint of stock, a quart of milk, and let boil until tender; cook half a pint of lentils in one pint of stock; when the strips of calves' feet are cooked, strain off the gravy into a stewpan, add a little roux and the juice of two lemons; let it boil, then sharply whisk in four eggs, and keep stirring until it boils; place the strips of feet on a hot dish, pour the sauce over them, and lay the lentils round them; garnish with croûtons o. fried bread.

MUTTON CUTLETS, SARDINIAN SAUCE.

Ingredients: About three pounds best end neck of mutton, two eggs, some breadcrumbs, four ounces butter, one pint of stock, one shalot, a little parsley, a tin of preserved mushrooms, eight Spanish olives cut in quarters, three ounces of lean ham, a little roux, a wineglassful of vinegar, and a little mushroom catsup. Saw off the chine and trim the mutton, then cut out the cutlets, flatten them with a cutlet-bat or chopper dipped in cold water, trim them into shape, dip them in two eggs beaten up with some seasoning, then in breadcrumbs; melt a little butter, pour it into a frying-pan, lay in the cutlets, and place away until dinner-time. Chop one shalot and a little parsley very fine, place them in a stewpan with some seasoning and one ounce butter; let fry five minutes; pour in one pint of stock, add a little roux; let boil ten minutes, then add one tin of preserved mushrooms left whole, eight Spanish olives cut in quarters, three ounces lean ham cut in small squares, the vinegar and mushroom catsup; let simmer gently one hour. Ten minutes before wanted, fry the cutlets a light brown, let them drain on a piece of paper before the fire, to absorb the butter; place them in a circle overlapping one another on a bed of mashed potatoes on a hot dish, and pour the boiling sauce over them. Serve immediately.

ROAST DUCKLINGS.

Cover the breasts of two fine ducklings with buttered paper, bake them in a hot oven thirty-five minutes; when cooked, place them on a very hot dish, and pour over them some good gravy seasoned and colored with a little soy.

SALAD.

Well wash and pick four lettuces, one endive, one punnet of small salad; free them from water by swinging them in a cloth; cut into moderate-sized pieces, place in a salad-bowl, and pour over the following sauce: Mix in a basin the yolks of two eggs, a little mustard, a little salt, a gill of olive oil, a gill of vinegar, and half a gill of cream; stir these ingredients well together, and pour over the salad; ornament the top of the salad with beet-root, cucumber, and hard-boiled eggs cut in slices.

MACARONI AU GRATIN.

Ingredients: One pound pipe macaroni, four ounces butter, some seasoning, half a pound grated cheese, (Parmesan and Cheddar,) a little grated nutmeg, one quart of milk, and a few breadcrumbs. Boil one pound macaroni in a quart of milk until tender, pour off the milk, and gently mix in the stewpan with the macaroni some seasoning, eight ounces grated cheese, and four ounces butter; place in a deep dish or shallow pie-dish, grate a little nutmeg over it, and lightly cover the top with breadcrumbs; place in a hot oven to brown, and serve immediately.

PINE SOUFFLÉ.

Ingredients: One pint of milk, four ounces butter, five ounces flour, five ounces powdered white sugar, five eggs, and a small tin of preserved pineapple. Into a stewpan put one pint of milk and four ounces butter; allow it to boil, then stir in the flour, and mix into a smooth compact paste; let the paste get nearly cold, crush the pineapple with five ounces sugar in the mortar, then stir it in the paste, add the yolks of five eggs, and well mix them in with a wooden spoon; whisk up the five whites to a firm snow, and stir lightly in the paste mixture; turn in a well-buttered soufflé-basin, place a band of paper round it, and bake in a good oven one hour. When required for table, take off the paper band, put a folded napkin round it, and send to table immediately.

ASPARAGUS WITH BROWNED BUTTER.

Scrape the asparagus quite clean, wash it in a pan of cold water, tie it in bundles of about eighteen to twenty in each, keeping all the heads turned the same way; cut the stalks even, leaving them about seven to eight inches in length; put the asparagus in hot water, with a small handful of salt in it, to boil for about twenty-five minutes, and, when done, drain carefully upon a napkin, to avoid breaking off the heads; dish on a square piece of toasted bread, and pour over the following: Place in a stewpan three ounces fresh butter, a little seasoning and grated nutmeg; place on the stove, and let boil until it assumes a light golden brown; (take care not to let it burn) then pour over the asparagus, and serve very hot.

SAVORY POT.

Take the pieces of cold meat and cut them to the size of dice, lay them in a pie-dish, and sprinkle over them a little pepper, salt, and two chopped onions; add two cloves, a teaspoonful or two of dry sage, or a small bunch of sweet herbs. Thicken about a teacupful of thin stock with a little flour, and pour over, then cover all with potatoes cut in thick slices, and bake for an hour. The potatoes should be half boiled first. This is a very economical dish, and is as nice cold as hot.

BEEF STEAK WITH MACARONI.

One pound beef steak cut half an inch thick, well beaten with a rolling-pin; one onion sliced and put into a frying-pan with one ounce of dripping, and fried a nice brown color; take three ounces of macaroni and put into some boiling water and a little salt, and boil for ten minutes; put a cup of hot water on a piece of crust of bread made *very* brown, and let it stand ten minutes, then pour the water on to the onion and keep hot until the meat is done; now sprinkle the steak with pepper, salt and flour, and put in a frying-pan over a good fire; in five minutes turn the meat and fry five minutes on the other side; take it up, pour the onion into the pan and make quite hot; add a spoonful of catsup and pour over the steak, and put the macaroni round. This is a most excellent dish.

BRAISED STEAK À LA LOTTA.

One pound of lean, tender beef steak fried lightly in a little dripping; fry with it an onion, four ounces weight, cut small; drain them from the fat and put into a baking-dish or jar, with half pint of water; add a grated carrot, a small one; pepper and salt and four cloves; tablespoonful Yorkshire relish, same quantity of vinegar, a small lump of sugar; stew slowly until tender, about one and a-half hours; thicken with browned flour, or, if preferred, a tablespoonful of rice added as soon as the gravy begins to simmer; a few drops of browning or a little browning salt improves it.

BRAISED STEAK À LA CONEY ISLAND.

Take one pound steak, fry in a little butter to a rich brown, then put it into a saucepan well covered with water, and add the following ingredients: One onion chopped rather fine; two carrots, ditto; two turnips, ditto; one blade of mace, a touch of nutmeg, one clove, pepper and salt to taste; simmer gently for two hours; thicken with a tablespoonful of flour; have ready a hot dish, on which strew a little chopped parsley; pour over the steak and serve.

BEEF STEAK, LONG BRANCH STYLE.

Cut one pound steak off either rump or sirloin of beef, (you may leave it whole or divide into nice pieces,) dip in salad oil, and put aside for a few hours, until it is required; then broil over a clear fire, and serve with sauce made as follows: Put a piece of butter, size of a walnut, in a saucepan, with some finely-chopped onion and parsley; add a little lemon-juice, pepper and salt; stir on the fire for five minutes, and serve very hot.

While congratulating all my fair correspondents upon their attempts to carry off the prize, and regretting my inability to give many of them more substantial reward than praise, I beg leave to present to them my own recipe.

STEAK À LA DUCHESSE.

Trim the steak, making it into a fair oval or round. Cut off altogether not less than a quarter of a pound. Run all that is cut off through a mincing-machine twice; add to the mince an equal amount of breadcrumbs, an uncooked onion chopped very fine, and a small pinch of some fine herb most agreeable to the taste. I prefer sage, and some pepper and salt; mix thoroughly, then put into a brazing-pan, with a small lump of butter, and let it brown well. If put on the fire about five minutes before the steak, and kept well stirred, both will be done together. Take one egg, a tablespoonful of salad oil, a tablespoonful of white wine or Taragon vinegar, a little mustard, or some grated horseradish, if it is to be had; and beat up the whole well. Heat, but do not boil: this in a little saucepan. When the steak is broiled sufficiently, (it should not be overdone,) put into a hot dish, place the mince all round it, and if mashed potatoes are served, put them as an outer wall all round the mince. Just before serving, pour the sauce gently on to the centre of the steak.

STEAK AUX LEGUMES.

Take a pound of steak, not too fat, cut thick; insert a sharp-pointed knife in the edge and divide in two, with the exception of a small space round the edge. The steak should now form a sort of bag. Care should be taken to keep the external opening as small as possible. Have ready two small onions cut in slices and fried a nice brown; also a fried mushroom minced finely. Put the onions and mushroom, with a little salt and pepper, into the opening made, (taking care to preserve the original shape of the steak,) and grill over a clear fire for five or seven minutes, turning with the tongs, and being careful to catch the gravy. Take a carrot, cut it in slices of an inch long, and with a sharp knife cut each of these as if peeling them round and round in a continuous strip, so as to form a ribbon; cut a turnip in the same way. Boil these carefully, and when the steak is sufficiently cooked, put it on a hot dish, pour over it the gravy, and garnish with ribbons of carrot and turnip.

SOUP À LA CONNAUGHT.

Ingredients: Five pounds lean beef, three onions, three carrots, one head of celery, a little parsley, a sprig of thyme, two blades of mace, a few allspice, some seasoning, a little soy, five quarts of water, tin of preserved peas, two ounces rice, and four ounces lean ham. Cut up the onions, carrots and celery into pieces, and lay them on the bottom of a stewpan; cut the beef into small pieces, and place on the top of the vegetables; sprinkle some pepper and salt over it, and stand it on the stove to cook the meat for about one hour, then add five quarts of water, and let it boil; take off the scum as it rises, and add half a pint of cold water, a little soy, a little parsley, a sprig of thyme, a few allspice, and two blades of mace, and let all simmer together for four hours; strain the soup through a fine cloth, and take off any remaining fat with a piece of paper laid lightly on the soup. Cook two ounces rice in boiling water until tender, make a tin of peas hot by standing in boiling water, and cut four ounces lean cooked ham into very fine dice, and place in the tureen with the rice and peas; pour the boiling soup over them, and serve immediately.

POTATO SOUP À LA CREME.

Ingredients: Four pounds of potatoes, two quarts of milk, one onion, one head of celery, two blades of mace, one pound of veal, three ounces of butter, one lemon, one quart of water, a gill of cream, and some seasoning. Into a large stewpan put three ounces butter, one onion, and one head of celery cut into slices, one pound veal. Place the stewpan on the stove, and let cook gently for twenty minutes; peel the potatoes, and cut them into thin slices, and place in the stewpan with the cooked vegetables and veal; add one quart of water, the rind of one lemon, some seasoning, and two quarts of milk, and let it simmer gently two hours (occasionally stirring to prevent its burning); pass the soup through a fine hair sieve into a clean stewpan, and stand it in some boiling water to keep hot; before sending to table, add a gill of cream, and season to taste; send with the soup some small croutons of fried bread.

FILLETS OF BRILL, POLISH SAUCE.

Ingredients: Four fillets of brill, two lemons, one onion, one carrot, some seasoning, a handful of parsley, a stick of horse-radish, a little anchovy sauce, one ounce sugar, one pint of stock, and a little roux. Cut each fillet into three pieces, and lay them in a well-buttered baking-tin, sprinkle some seasoning over them, and squeeze the juice of two lemons over them; cover with a piece of buttered paper, and bake in a hot oven twenty minutes. Into a stewpan put a piece of butter about the size of a walnut, one onion, and one carrot cut into slices, and some seasoning; place on the stove and lightly fry, then add a little anchovy sauce, one pint of stock, one ounce sugar, and a little roux; boil all together for twenty minutes, then strain through a fine hair sieve; to the sauce add a handful of parsley blanched and chopped very fine, and one horseradish scraped very fine; let the sauce boil a few minutes; dish the fillets in a circle overlapping one another, and pour the boiling sauce over them, and serve very hot.

DRESSED SALMON, ITALIAN SAUCE.

Ingredients: Two slices of middle cut of salmon, about one and a-half pounds to two pounds in weight each, three onions, two carrots, two blades of mace, a few allspice, two shalots, a tin of preserved mushrooms, one bay-leaf, a sprig of thyme, some seasoning, a little parsley, one pint of stock, and a little roux. Cut up three onions, two carrots, (very thin,) and place them in a baking-dish; add a few allspice, two blades of mace, and some seasoning; then lay the slices of salmon on the top of the vegetables, and cover with a piece of buttered paper, and bake in a hot oven thirty minutes. Into a stewpan put one pint of stock, a sprig of thyme, a bay-leaf, a little piece of carrot, an onion, and a little roux; boil together twenty minutes, and strain through a fine hair-sieve. Chop very finely two shalots, and put them into a stewpan with two ounces butter, and let them simmer a few minutes; then add a tin of preserved mushrooms chopped fine, and a little finely-chopped parsley; let all simmer a few minutes, then pour in the sauce, add seasoning to taste, and a little soy to color it brown; lift the slices of salmon very carefully on to a hot dish, take care not to allow any of the vegetables to remain on them, and pour the boiling sauce over them; then squeeze the juice of a lemon over them, and serve immediately.

BOILED CHICKENS, BECHEMEL SAUCE.

Ingredients: Two chickens, one pint of milk, one onion, one carrot, a stick of celery, a blade of mace, some seasoning, a little roux, and a gill of cream. Have a stewpan large enough to hold the chickens, put in half an onion, half a carrot, a little piece of celery, a pinch of sugar, the same of salt, and then lay in the chickens; prick them all over the breast with a needle, and cover them with boiling water, and boil steadily for thirty-five minutes. Into a stewpan put one pint of milk, a piece of onion, a piece of carrot, a piece of celery, a blade of mace, some seasoning, and a little roux, enough to thicken it; boil twenty minutes, and strain through a fine hair sieve; add a gill of cream, and bring to the boil; place the fowls in a very hot dish, take out the skewers, and wipe away any moisture with a clean napkin; then pour a little sauce over them, and garnish with some slices of lemon and green parsley; serve the rest of the sauce in a boat.

BRAISED HAM À LA CINTRA.

Ingredients: A Westphalia or York ham, about ten pounds in weight, (if chosen smaller, they are drier, and eat rough,) three onions, three carrots, one head of celery, two bay-leaves, a handful of parsley, a small bunch of sweet herbs, some seasoning, one pound rice, four ounces butter, a little tomato sauce, some breadcrumbs, and a tin of preserved green peas. Soak the ham for twelve hours, then scrape it clean, and trim it; place it in a braising-pan, with the onions, carrots and celery cut into small pieces; add two bay-leaves, a bunch of sweet herbs, some pepper, and a handful of parsley; cover the ham with cold water, and let it come to the boil; then, if possible, put the pot in the oven and braise five hours. Chop up one onion and a piece of celery very finely, place it in a stewpan with four ounces butter, and let simmer fifteen minutes; then add to it one pint of the liquor from the ham-braise, free from fat, one pint of water, and one pound rice well washed and picked, and let simmer until the rice is tender; then add a small bottle of tomato sauce and a tin of preserved green peas; mix all gently together and set on the stove in not too hot a place. Take the ham out of the braise, then trim off the rind and rough fat; cover it with brown breadcrumbs, put a frill on the knuckle, and place the ham on a very hot dish, and place the rice garniture round it, and serve very hot.

MUTTON CUTLETS À LA GODIVEAN.

Ingredients: Best end neck of mutton, one onion, one carrot, a little celery, one quart of stock, some seasoning, one tin of preserved mushrooms, four eggs, half a pint of milk, four ounces flour, four ounces lean ham. Trim the mutton and cut out the cutlets, (twelve in number,) cut up the onion, carrot and celery into thin slices, and place them in a stewpan; lay in the cutlets in a circle on the top of the vegetables; add one quart of stock and some seasoning, and let simmer forty minutes; then take the cutlets and lay them on some clean white paper and place between two tins, with a weight on the top to press them; when quite cold, trim them into shape and place in the larder until ten minutes before wanted. Reduce the gravy that the cutlets were cooked in to one-half by boiling, take off the fat, and add one tin of preserved mushrooms and four ounces cooked lean ham cut into small squares, and let simmer together twenty minutes. Just before dinner-time, mix four ounces flour, a little milk and the yolks of four eggs well together; add some seasoning; well whisk four whites of eggs into a firm snow, and stir lightly in the batter; dip the cutlets in the batter and drop them into a stewpan of boiling lard or dripping, and fry them a light golden brown; when fried, drain them on some clean paper to absorb the fat; place a little bed of mashed potatoes in a hot entrée-dish, and dish the cutlets in a circle, overlapping one another on it; pour the sauce in the centre, and serve very hot.

BLANQUETTE OF VEAL À LA REFORM.

Ingredients: Veal, mushrooms, gherkins, one onion, one carrot, one head of celery, a little parsley, some seasoning, one quart of stock, a little roux, two eggs, three ounces butter, and half a pound of rice. Take a piece of cold roast veal and cut it into scollops about an inch and a half long and a quarter inch thick; sprinkle them with seasoning, and lay them in a stewpan with a tin of preserved mushrooms and eight gherkins cut into long strips. Cut one onion, one carrot, one head of celery into small pieces, place them into a stewpan with one quart of stock, a little parsley, and some seasoning, and simmer for one hour; then add a little roux, and strain through a fine metal strainer; put into a stewpan three ounces butter and two eggs, and whisk in the boiling sauce; let come to the boil, and pour over the scollops, and stand it in not too hot a place on the stove. Well pick and wash half a pound of rice, throw it into boiling water with a pinch of salt, and boil until tender; then strain it in a hair sieve until free from moisture, and while still hot fill a buttered mould having a large hole in the centre, turn the rice out on a hot dish, and fill the centre with the scollops, and serve very hot.

BEEF OLIVES, SHERRY SAUCE.

Ingredients: Two pounds rump steak, half a pound sausages, a little parsley, a bunch of sweet herbs, one onion, one carrot, a few allspice, a bay-leaf, a little celery, some seasoning, one quart of stock, a little roux, one egg, one tin of preserved mushrooms, and some mashed potatoes. Cut the steak in twelve thin slices, and beat them very thin with a cutlet-bat dipped in water, and spread them with a farce made as follows: Mix together half a pound sausages, one egg, a handful of parsley chopped very fine, and a little finely-rubbed thyme and some seasoning; then roll them up and tie a piece of string round them, and place them in a frying-pan with a little butter, and fry them a light brown all over; when fried, place them in a stewpan with a small bunch of sweet herbs, one onion, one carrot, a little celery cut into pieces, one bay-leaf, a few allspice, and a quart of stock; let simmer one hour, strain off the gravy and thicken it with a little roux; add a little soy, and strain through a fine metal strainer; add a tin of preserved mushrooms to the sauce, and bring to the boil; take off the scum as it rises. Trim the olives and take off the string, and place them in a circle in a bed of mashed potatoes, and pour the boiling sauce over them, and serve immediately.

GUINEA FOWL.

Ingredients: Two guinea fowls, a piece of fat bacon, one onion, half a pint of milk, some seasoning, a few breadcrumbs, a pint of good stock, and two bunches of watercresses. Lard the breasts of two guinea fowls, and roast them before a good fire for forty minutes, well basting them with butter or dripping; make bread-sauce as follows: Boil half a pint of milk, put in one small onion stuck with cloves, some seasoning, and a handful of breadcrumbs, and let boil gently ten minutes; take out the onion, and the sauce is ready; dish the fowls in a hot dish, pour over them some boiling gravy, and place round them two bunches of watercresses, and serve the bread-sauce in a boat.

PLOVERS.

Ingredients: Five plovers, some gravy, five pieces of toast, a piece of fat bacon. Cover the breasts of the plovers with thin slices of fat bacon, and roast for twenty minutes before a sharp, clear fire, occasionally basting with some dripping; place some pieces of toast under them to catch the trail whilst roasting; put the plovers on a hot dish, take out the skewers and pieces of fat from off them, and pour some melted butter over them. and place the pieces of trailed toast round them; serve some boiling gravy in a sauce-tureen.

CHEESE FONDU.

Ingredients: One pint of milk, five ounces butter, some seasoning, five ounces flour, six ounces Parmesan cheese, six eggs. Into a stewpan put one pint of milk and five ounces butter, and some seasoning, and let it boil one minute; then add five ounces good flour, and stir on the fire until the paste leaves the stewpan quite free; then stir in the yolks of six eggs and six ounces grated Parmesan cheese, and mix well together; whisk up the six whites to a strong snow, and mix lightly in the batter; place in a fondu basin, place a band of paper round it, and bake in a hot oven fifty minutes; serve the fondu on a napkin.

CHESTERFIELD PUDDING.

Ingredients: Four ounces butter, six ounces sugar, six eggs, five ounces breadcrumbs, four ounces flour, three ounces sultanas, one ounce dried cherries, and two ounces fine-chopped lemon-peel, one glass of brandy, one glass of port wine, the rind of one lemon, and a little essence of almonds. Slightly warm the butter in a basin, and with a wooden spoon beat to a cream; then beat in four ounces powdered white sugar, and add one egg at a time, until all six are worked in; then stir in the flour, breadcrumbs and fruit; mix lightly all together, and put the mixture in a buttered mould dusted with flour, and steam two hours; when cooked, turn the mould into a hot dish, and pour over it the following mixture: Melt two ounces sugar in a tablespoonful of water, grate in the rind of one lemon, and add one glass of brandy and the same of port wine. Serve the pudding very hot.

MUSHROOMS AU GRATIN.

Ingredients: Mushrooms, parsley, ham, butter, gravy, bread crumbs, seasoning, thyme, and four eggs. Cut the stalks, and trim the edges of the mushrooms, (about two punnets are enough for a good dish,) and fill them with the following mixture: Chop up four ounces lean ham and a handful of parsley very fine; put them in a stewpan with one ounce butter and a pinch of flour, some seasoning, and a little finely-rubbed thyme, and place on the fire and make thoroughly hot; then stir in four eggs until the mixture forms a thick custard. When the mushrooms are filled, place them in a shallow stewpan with some butter and a little gravy, cover with breadcrumbs, and place in a hot oven for fifteen minutes to gratinate; when cooked, dish them up in a heap in the centre of a hot dish, and pour some boiling well-seasoned gravy round them.

DUCHESSE LOAVES WITH APPLE JELLY.

Ingredients: Half a pint of milk, four ounces butter, two ounces sugar, five ounces flour, four eggs, and a little rough sugar candy. Put the milk, sugar and butter into a stewpan on the fire, and as soon as these begin to boil, stir in five ounces flour; when thoroughly mixed, add three eggs; incorporate these with the paste. This paste should now be laid out with a dessert spoon in heaps about the size of a small egg; egg them over with a brush, and strew a little coarsely-crushed sugar-candy over them, and bake them in a moderate oven a very light color; when baked, make an incision in the side with a sharp knife, and put in them a little apple jelly. Send to table on a napkin.

CHERRY JELLY.

Ingredients: Two ounces Nelson's opaque gelatine, four lemons, half a pound sugar, one pint and a half of water, the whites of three eggs, half a glass of noyeau, one drop of essence of almonds, and a little cochineal. Soak the gelatine in the water for one hour, then add the juice of four lemons, the sugar, and the whites of three eggs whisked in a little cold water; stir all together gently over the fire until boiling; let it settle a few minutes, then pass through a flannel jelly-bag, pouring it back a few times, until quite clear; then add half a glass of noyeau, one drop of essence of almonds, and color a light red with cochineal. Pour into a mould and let set; when required, dip the mould in warm water for a few seconds, and wipe with a cloth and turn on to a glass or silver dish.

EGYPTIAN CREAM.

Ingredients: Half a pint of cream, one lemon, half a glass

of noyeau, one ounce isinglass, a little cochineal, half a pint of clear jelly, the same as the foregoing recipe. Pour the clear jelly into a plain mould and let it set; when set, turn it out on to a dish, and keep very cold. Whisk up half a pint of cream very stiff, then divide it into two parts, (one flavor lemon, the other noyeau,) colored with cochineal; dissolve one ounce isinglass in a little hot water, and add half of it to the lemon cream; well whisk in with a little finely-powdered sugar, and pour in the mould the jelly was turned out of; when set, turn it out on to a dish, then sweeten the noyeau cream, add the dissolved isinglass, and set in the mould the lemon was turned out of; then cut each layer into six pieces, and work them alternately back into the mould; pour in a little liquid jelly and let set; turn out the same as before described.

CROQUETTES OF POTATOES.

Take one quart of finely-mashed potatoes, place in a basin, season with pepper and salt and a teaspoonful of parsley chopped very fine, one egg, one ounce of liquid butter. Beat this mixture well. Flour a board slightly, divide the mixture into small portions, shape them like apples and pears. Any lady having artistic taste can model these beautifully out of the potato paste. Egg and breadcrumb the croquettes, place in a frying-basket and fry for four minutes; drain, and place a clove in the top of each apple and pear, and a small stalk of parsley in the other end of the fruit. This is a very pretty dish.

RISSOLES

Are portions of highly-seasoned cooked meat, fish, or game, enclosed in pastry, and fried. Very good rissoles can be made by using a small quantity of tinned meat. Of course the rissoles will be nicer if cold roast meat, roast fowl or game is used. Any sort of cold meat will do. Season the meat nicely, and, if it is not very juicy, add a small quantity of stock to it. For one dozen rissoles, take one pound cooked meat nicely minced and seasoned, tablespoonful of stock; mix well; form the mixture into small corks. Prepare a paste of half a pound of flour, four ounces of butter, a pinch of salt, half a teaspoonful of baking-powder, and one gill of water. Place flour in a basin, rub the butter into the flour, add salt, baking-powder and water; mix well; turn paste out on the board and roll out thinly, say half an inch in thickness; cut into small rounds with a cutter or a tumbler; lay a little cork of the meat on the round of paste. Brush the edges of the paste, fold the paste over so as to form a half-moon shape, press the edges well together, place the rissoles in a plate with beaten egg, brush well all over, then roll them in breadcrumbs and fry in fat about three hundred and seventy-five degrees, so as to get the pastry nicely raised. The pastry becomes light, and the rissoles float on the surface of the fat after the first minute, so they must be moved about with a slice, so as to get them evenly browned. Rissoles will require about six minutes to fry.

Croquettes of rice, fritters, and potato chips, can be fried easily by this process. The secret of success of frying is to have plenty of fat, more than enough to cover the things to be fried, to see that the fat is hot, and that articles intended to be fried are well egged and breadcrumbed. Potato chips do not require egg and breadcrumbs; they may be rolled in a small quantity of flour before they are fried, and ought to be well sprinkled with salt after they are fried and drained. Many sorts of cheap fish can be fried after they have been well rolled in flour or oatmeal.

ORANGE JELLY.

Dissolve one ounce Nelson's opaque gelatine in one pint of cold water for two hours, then add eight ounces white sugar, the juice of one lemon, and half a pint of boiling water; place on the fire until the gelatine is all melted, add the juice of five oranges and one drop of cochineal, strain through a piece of muslin and pour into a mould, and put into a cool place to set. When wanted, dip the mould into warm water for a few seconds, wipe dry with a clean cloth, and turn gently into a silver or glass dish. Ornament with a few natural flowers, if procurable.

SAVARIN OF GREENGAGES WITH WHIPT CREAM.

Take half a pint of milk, make it warm, add four ounces sugar, and one-half ounce German yeast, and two ounces flour; well mix together, and stand in a warm place to rise; then put one pound flour on the paste-board, rub in one-half pound butter, bring into a heap in the centre of the board, and with the hand scoop a hole in the centre; then place in the hollow the yolks of five eggs, and a glass of noyeau and the ferment; mix into a smooth compact dough, add four ounces picked sultanas, a few dried cherries, and a little chopped mixed peel; well butter a large mould having a hollow in the centre, three parts fill the mould with the dough, and then stand it in a warm place to prove; when it has risen near the top of the mould, place a band of buttered paper round it, and bake in a moderate oven for about forty minutes, more or less, according to the heat of the oven; when cooked, turn out of the mould, and let get partly cold; fill the hollow with a tin of greengages preserved in syrup, and on the top put a little whipt cream, and just before sending to table, throw a few nonpareils on the top of the cream.

RUSSIAN SALAD.

Take about eight medium-sized potatoes, nicely boiled and floury; peel, and while hot, with a silver fork break them into little pieces about the size of small nuts. Boil hard about five or six eggs, chop the yolks and whites separately; take about half a tumbler of best Lucca oil, a little vinegar, pepper, salt, capers; a couple of chopped anchovies, if for a fish salad, or the liver of a fowl bruised in the sauce, if for fowl, is a great improvement; if the latter, chop the meat into small pieces; or, if fish, shred it into little bits. Take half the eggs and mix with the sauce, place it in the dish you intend serving it in; smooth the surface, cover it lightly with the remainder of the chopped eggs, and garnish with pickles and beet-root.

ALMA PUDDING.

Beat one-quarter pound butter to a thick cream, strew in by degrees one-half pound sugar, and beat these well together; then dredge one-half pound flour in gradually, add one-quarter pound currants, and then beat up four eggs and add them to the mixture; when all the ingredients are well stirred and mixed, pour into a buttered mould and tie down with a cloth ; put the pudding into a saucepan with boiling water, and let it boil for four hours.

FIG PUDDING.

Chop one-half pound figs very finely, mix them with one-quarter pound coarse sugar, a tablespoonful of treacle, four tablespoonfuls of milk, one-half pound flour, one-quarter pound suet, an egg, and a pinch of grated nutmeg. Put the pudding into a buttered mould and boil five hours.

SCRAP PUDDING.

Put scraps of bread (crust and crumb) into a bowl, with sufficient milk to cover them well. Cover with a plate, and put into the oven to soak for about half an hour. Take it out and mash the bread with a fork till it is a pulp; then add a handful of raisins and as many currants, six ounces brown sugar, half a pint of milk, some candied lemon-peel, and one egg. Stir it up well, grease a pudding-dish, and pour the pudding in. Grate over a little nutmeg, put it into a moderate oven, and let it bake for an hour and a-half.

SCOTCH CAKE.

Stir to a cream one pound sugar, three-quarters pound butter, add the grated rind and juice of a lemon; separate the whites and yolks of nine eggs and beat each to a froth; stir into the cake, and add one pound sifted flour; stir fifteen minutes, and just before putting into cake-pans, which must be lined with buttered paper, add one pound raisins; spice to taste, and bake one hour.

CELERY SAUCE.

Cut up a large bunch of celery into small pieces; use only that which is blanched. Put it into a pint of water and boil until it is tender; then add a teaspoonful of flour and a lump of butter the size of an egg, mixed well together; season with salt and pepper, and stir constantly until taken from the fire. It is very nice with boiled poultry.

MAIDS OF HONOR.

Beat one pound powdered loaf sugar with the yolks of twelve eggs in a mortar, one ounce blanched sweet almonds, and twelve bitter, and four tablespoonfuls of orange-flower water; the almonds must be mixed in just before the patty-pans are filled. Line your patty-pans with good puff-paste, put in the mixture, and bake in a moderately-heated oven.

TO MAKE A TRIFLE.

The whip to put over the trifle should be made the day before it is required, as keeping it for a day improves the flavor, and makes it more solid. Put into a large bowl three ounces pounded loaf sugar, the whites of two eggs, one pint of cream, and a small glass of sherry or raisin wine. Whisk these ingredients well in a cool place, and take off the froth with a skimmer as fast as it rises, and put it on a sieve to drain; continue the whisking until there is sufficient of the whip, which must be put away in a cool place to drain. For the trifle, place six small spongecakes, twelve macaroons, and two dozen ratafias at the bottom of the trifle-dish; pour over them half a pint of sherry or sweet wine, mixed with six tablespoonfuls of brandy, or, if this is considered too much, a little less brandy and more wine; the cakes should be well soaked. Over the cakes put the grated rind of a lemon, about two or three ounces sweet almonds blanched and cut into strips, and a layer of raspberry or strawberry jam; make a good custard and pour over the cakes; then heap the whip lightly over the top as high as possible, and garnish with strips of bright currant jelly, crystallized sweetmeats or flowers.

ORANGE MARMALADE.

Allow the same weight of lump sugar as of oranges; cut the oranges in half and take out the inside, removing the pips and skin that separates the quills, leaving only the juice and pulp. Wash the inside skin in a little water, and put it to your pulp; the rinds must be boiled about four hours in plenty of water, changing it once, or it will be too bitter; when sufficiently boiled, cut in small pieces. Next boil the pulp, juice and sugar together for half an hour, then put in the pieces of rind, and boil for four or five minutes.

SOUP A LA ROYALE.

Cut up four onions, two carrots and one head of celery into small pieces, and lay them in the bottom of a large stewpan; then lay in five pounds lean beef cut into small pieces, sprinkle with pepper and salt, and place the stewpan on a slow fire and cook for one hour, (taking care it does not burn); then add four quarts of cold water, let it boil, take off the scum and fat, and add one bay-leaf, a few allspice and a bunch of herbs, a little soy and a very little cayenne pepper, and let simmer four hours; strain through a cloth, and take off the fat with a piece of clean paper laid lightly on the soup; take the yolks of six eggs, add to them a tablespoonful of milk, some pepper and salt, well whisk all together, and pour into a buttered mould and steam fifteen minutes; when done, cut the custard into small diamond-shaped pieces and place in the tureen, pour the boiling soup over them and serve.

BISQUE OF RABBIT.

Cut up two rabbits, place them in a stewpan with one onion, one bay-leaf, a blade of mace, a small piece of celery, some seasoning, and two quarts of stock-broth; boil together until the rabbits are tender, take them out of the gravy, save the best pieces of meat for sending in the soup to table, pound the bones in a mortar with a little grated nutmeg, then put them back in the gravy; add one quart of milk and a little roux, and boil twenty minutes; strain through a fine hair sieve, add the pieces of meat cut into small squares, and a little chopped parsley, and the juice of one lemon; bring to the boil, take off the scum, and the soup is ready for serving.

EELS À LA TARTARE.

Procure three pounds eels, place them in a hot oven for ten minutes, remove the skins, and cut them into pieces about two inches long, and lay them in a little well-seasoned stock, and boil gently twenty minutes; put into a stewpan one pint of milk, two ounces butter, and a little roux; boil together five minutes, add some seasoning, the juice of one lemon, a gill of white vinegar, and four eggs; well whisk together until boiling, then add one ounce capers chopped fine, and a little chopped parsley; lift the pieces of eels gently out of the stewpan, and place in a heap in the centre of a hot dish and pour the sauce over. Garnish with some croutons of fried bread, and serve.

WHITINGS AU GRATIN.

Procure five whitings, place them in a baking-dish with a gill of good gravy, sprinkle over them a little chopped shalot and parsley, some seasoning, and a little anchovy sauce; add the juice of two lemons and half a gill of cream; cover with buttered paper, and bake in a hot oven twenty minutes; then take off the paper and sprinkle over the fish a few breadcrumbs, and set in the oven to brown. Serve in the dish they are baked in, with a napkin round it, and in a boat send a sauce made as follows: Half a pint of good stock, some seasoning, a little anchovy sauce, and a glass of port, boiled together; thicken with a little roux, and strain through a fine hair sieve.

CAPON À LA REINE.

Take one large or two small capons, rub them over with half a lemon, and then wrap them in white paper, and place them in a stewpan, with enough good stock to cover them; add one onion, a head of celery, and a small carrot cut into pieces, a blade of mace, and a little grated nutmeg, and let simmer for one hour and a quarter just before dinner-time; take out the capons and let them drain upon a napkin. Boil some very small turnips in water, with a pinch of sugar and the same of salt, and one ounce butter, until tender; boil some Brussels sprouts very green. Take some of the gravy the capon was cooked in, thicken it with a little roux, and add a gill of cream to it; strain it through a fine hair sieve; place the capon on a hot dish, and put round it in little heaps, alternately, the turnips and Brussels sprouts; pour the boiling sauce over it, and serve immediately.

CALF'S HEAD À LA D'ORLEANS.

Take the scalp off the head and well wash it, wipe it dry with a cloth, and cover it with a farce made as follows: Two pounds sausage-meat, a handful of breadcrumbs, a little chopped parsley, a little grated nutmeg, some seasoning, and three eggs mixed together; spread this evenly over the head, and roll up tightly and tie in a cloth; place it in a stewpan with two onions, one carrot, and one head of celery, a few allspice, and some seasoning, and two quarts of stock-broth, and boil gently three hours. Chop up ten gherkins very fine, and place them in a stewpan with some seasoning and two eggs, and stir them well together over a good fire for ten minutes. When the calf's head is cooked, carefully turn out of the cloth and spread the gherkin-mixture over the top with the blade of a knife. Take some of the gravy the head was cooked in, and thicken it with a little roux; add a little soy and two glasses of sherry; bring to the boil, and strain through a fine hair sieve. Pare ten carrots and five turnips, and cut them into small square pieces and boil them separately in salt and water, with a pinch of sugar added, until tender; strain them and keep very hot. Place the head carefully, with a large fish-slice, on a hot dish, and pour the boiling sauce over it, and lay in little heaps alternately the carrots and turnips round it; sprinkle a little chopped parsley on the turnips, and serve immediately.

SUPREME OF CHICKEN À LA MARÉCHALE.

Cut up two chickens into nice joints, throw them into lukewarm water with a pinch of salt added, and let them blanch for ten minutes, then drain them dry, dip them in flour, and fry a light brown in a little butter. Take one quart of milk and the same of stock, place in a stewpan with one onion, one carrot, a few allspice, a blade of mace, some seasoning, and a little grated nutmeg; boil together forty minutes, thicken with a little roux, and strain through a fine hair sieve; place the joints of chicken in the sauce, add a tin of preserved mushrooms and a glass of sherry, simmer together for forty minutes; place in a stewpan a tin of preserved green peas, a little seasoning, one ounce butter, and a little grated nutmeg, make a border round each entrée-dish with some mashed potatoes, place the supreme in the centre, and place the peas round the potato border, and then the entrée is ready.

GRENADINES OF VEAL A LA REGENCE.

Take about two pounds veal cutlet, cut it into twelve fillets, beat them flat with a cutlet-bat dipped in cold water, trim them into shape, and lard them with fat bacon; cut up one onion and one carrot into a flat stewpan, add a few blades of mace and a few allspice, then cover with some thin slices of fat bacon, and lay in the grenadines on the top of all; grate a little nutmeg over them, add some seasoning and sufficient stock-broth to reach up to the larding, and simmer gently for one hour. Well wash eight ounces Carolina rice, and throw into boiling water and let boil ten minutes, drain it dry, and then place it in a stewpan with one pint of good stock and some seasoning, and a spoonful of tomato sauce, and simmer gently for twenty minutes; add four drops of cochineal, and thoroughly incorporate with the rice. Boil one pound Brussels sprouts in salt and water until tender, and drain very dry. Pour the gravy from the grenadines into a stewpan, and reduce to one-half by boiling. Equally divide the rice into two hot entrée-dishes, and place the grenadines in a circle overlapping one another, and place half the Brussels sprouts in each centre; pour the boiling sauce over them and serve immediately.

ROAST PTARMIGAN AND HERB SAUCE.

Procure two fine ptarmigan, wrap them in buttered paper, and place them in a baking-tin with one pint of good gravy; bake them in a hot oven twenty-five minutes; take off the buttered paper a few minutes before wanted, to allow the breasts to brown. Cut up of each a handful of parsley and small onions very fine, place them in a stewpan with two ounces butter, some seasoning, and a little grated nutmeg, and fry gently for five minutes, occasionally stirring with a wooden spoon; then add one pint of good stock, and simmer twenty minutes. Serve the ptarmigan on a very hot dish, with the gravy from the tin they were roasted in, and send the herb sauce in a boat with them.

WILD DUCK AND RED CURRANT JELLY SAUCE.

Procure two fat wild ducks, place them in a baking-tin, sprinkle the breasts with a little flour and seasoning, cover with a piece of buttered paper, and bake thirty minutes in a hot oven, removing the paper a few minutes before wanted, to allow the breasts to brown. Place in a stewpan one pint of stock-broth, one bay-leaf, a few allspice, a sprig of thyme, a small pot of red currant jelly, a little roux, and some seasoning; boil all together ten minutes, strain through a fine hair sieve, add a little soy and a glass of port wine. Dish the ducks on a hot dish, and pour some of the boiling sauce over them, and send the rest in a boat, and one lemon cut into small pieces on a plate to be handed round with the duck.

CHEESE STRAWS.

Mix together on a pasteboard one-half pound flour, five ounces butter, five ounces grated Parmesan cheese, two eggs, a pinch of mustard, and some seasoning into a stiff paste; sprinkle the pasteboard with flour, and roll out the paste to the thickness of the sixth of an inch; then cut it into strips five inches long and a quarter of an inch wide, lay these on a clean baking-tin and bake a light golden brown in a hot oven. Dish the straws on a napkin, in the form of a pyramid.

LEMON PUDDING.

Well butter a plain mould, place in the bottom a few dried cherries and a piece of green citron cut into strips, break into pieces eight penny spongecakes, and fill the mould with them; then break into a basin six eggs, well whisk them, add five ounces powdered white sugar, the rind of two lemons grated, and one pint of milk; well whisk together, and pour gently into the mould, twist a piece of buttered paper over the mould, place in a stewpan, and add sufficient water to reach half-way up the mould; let gently boil one hour, taking care to add a little water to make up the loss by boiling. Place in a stewpan six ounces white sugar, the grated rind of one lemon, and a little water; boil together ten minutes, add half a glass of brandy, and the sauce is ready. When the pudding is required, run a thin knife gently round the mould, and turn gently into the dish. Pour the sauce over and serve

BRAISED CELERY.

Take six good heads of celery, trim to about six inches in length, parboil them in water with a little salt about ten minutes, take them out and drain them in a cloth or hair sieve, then place in a stewpan with one pint of stock-broth, add a little grated nutmeg and some seasoning, and boil gently for one hour. When cooked, take out the heads with a slice, drain on a cloth, add a little roux to the gravy, and boil for a few minutes; place the celery in a hot dish and strain the boiling sauce over it, garnish the sides with some small pieces of well-buttered, fresh-made toast, and serve very hot.

BANANA CREAM.

Procure five ripe bananas, take off the skins and pound the fruit in a mortar with five ounces white sugar to a pulp. Beat up half a pint of good cream to a stiff froth, add the pounded bananas and half a glass of brandy and the juice of one lemon; mix well together, then add one-half ounce isinglass dissolved, a little boiling-water, gently whisk in and fill the mould, set in a cool place until wanted. When required, dip the mould in warm water for a few seconds, wipe with a cloth, and turn out into a glass or silver dish.

FRENCH PASTRY.

Roll out a sheet of puff-paste, a quarter of an inch thick, cut into diamond, round and square-shaped pieces, gather the four corners of the squares into the middle, and stamp with a small round cutter; stamp the diamonds and rounds with three very small round cutters placed side by side, lay all on a sheet of paper on a baking-tin, lightly dust with white powdered sugar, and bake in a hot oven about ten minutes, more or less, according to the heat; when baked, take off the paper and fill the marked places with different-colored jams and jellies; thus, in some, for variety, place greengage jam, yellow apple jelly, and red currant jelly; in others, apricot jam, raspberry jam, and some preserved fruits. Dish the pastry on lace papers, in silver or glass dishes, in the form of a pyramid.

MOCK VENISON.

Bone and skin a loin of mutton; stew the bones with two anchovies, one or two onions, a bunch of sweet herbs, some white pepper, mace, a crust of bread, and a carrot; strain it off and put in a stewpan, with the fat side of the mutton downward; then add half a pint of port wine, and let it stew till tender; brown it in the dripping-pan, and serve it in the sauce.

APPLE CUSTARD.

Peel and core eight large juicy apples, and boil them till tender, in clear water. Take them out and pulp them smooth through a sieve; add one-quarter pound sifted sugar and the grated rind of two lemons. Put the mixture into a deep dish, about half filling it; beat the yolks of four eggs light, and add half a teacupful of white sugar, and stir into a quart of sweet milk; stir this over the fire until it is quite thick, and let it cool; when cold, pour it over the apples. Whip the whites of the eggs to a stiff froth and pour over the top.

TO MASH TURNIPS.

After having been boiled very tender, and the water pressed thoroughly from them, put them into a saucepan, and stir constantly for some minutes over a gentle fire; add a little cream, salt, fresh butter, and pepper; continue to simmer and stir them for five minutes longer, and then serve them.

POTATO ROLLS.

When mashed potato is left from the table, add one or two eggs, according to quantity, a little salt, pepper, butter and flour. Mix into small balls, and bake three-quarters of an hour on a buttered pan. These rolls make a cheap but nice breakfast relish.

CHRISTMAS CAKE.

One pound flour, one-half pound almonds, one pound sugar, three-quarters pound butter, six eggs, two teaspoonfuls of cream-tartar, one teaspoonful of soda, and half teacup of milk. Beat the butter and sugar to a cream, add eggs and milk, in which dissolve the soda, put the cream of tartar in flour, beat this all well, and then stir in the blanched almonds;; line a cake-tin with well-buttered paper. Bake in a steady but not too hot oven.

BIRTHDAY CAKE.

Half pound butter, half pound sifted sugar, four eggs, one pound flour, half pound dried currants, half pound raisins, two ounces candied orange-peel or citron, twelve almonds, a teaspoonful of baking-powder, and a teaspoonful of mixed spice. Beat the butter and sugar to a cream, add the eggs well beaten, the flour, and the fruit picked and floured. When all are well mixed, stir in the baking-powder last. The almonds must be blanched and chopped, and the orange-peel or citron shredded fine. Mix very thoroughly; pour into a well-buttered tin lined with buttered paper, and bake four hours in a moderate oven. The cake may be iced, if desired.

LITTLE PLUM CAKES.

Two pounds flour, half pound sugar, four eggs, half pound butter, six spoonfuls of cream, and half pound currants. Mix the butter and sugar to a cream, first washing the butter in rose-water; add the eggs well beaten, then the cream a little warm, then the flour and currants, the latter well washed and dried; mix well, and make into small cakes, or bake in very small ound tin pans in a tolerably hot oven. Frost them, and put a sugar ornament on each one.

CITRON CAKE.

Twelve eggs, one pound sugar, one pound butter, the rind and juice of a lemon, one pound flour, a grated nutmeg. Cut two pounds citron into small, thin pieces, rub them in flour, and, just before baking, add the citron to the cake-batter.; divide in two parts, and bake in a rather quick oven in well-buttered moulds.

COCOANUT PUFFS.

The whites of three eggs beaten very light, a teacupful of fine white sugar, a tablespoonful of corn-flour. When these ingredients are mixed, put the mixture into a custard saucepan or a jug, set in a pan of boiling water, and stir constantly for twenty minutes; then take it off the stove and add one-quarter pound grated cocoanut. When well mixed, drop in teaspoonfuls on buttered paper. Bake in a very slow oven, as they must not brown at all.

SUGAR PUFFS.

Take the whites of four eggs and beat them to a strong froth, a d add as much very fine rolled and sifted sugar as will make it into a stiff paste; add a few caraway seeds, a little rosewater or lemon essence to flavor the mixture. Beat it well for one hour, and then sift sugar on a sheet of white paper, and drop the mixture on it the size of a sixpence. Bake them carefully in a slow oven, and they will be very white.

LITTLE ALMOND CAKES.

Four ounces sweet almonds and four or five bitter ones, three-quarters pound flour, one pound sugar powdered and sifted, six ounces butter, and the yolk of one egg. Pound the almonds, rub the butter into the flour, and then mix all well together. Bake in buttered tins.

SCOLLOPS OF SWEETBREADS À LA VILLEROI.

Procure a pair of sweetbreads, blanch them in lukewarm water, changing the water two or three times, then throw them into some stock, and boil thirty minutes. Take out the sweetbreads and let them get cold, then cut into slices, egg and breadcrumb them, and fry them in a little clarified butter a golden brown. Thicken the gravy they were cooked in with a little roux, add two glasses of sherry, a bunch of herbs, and let simmer twenty minutes; then strain through a fine mesh metal strainer, add a tin of preserved mushrooms, boil some turnips quite tender, mash them, adding two boiled potatoes to stiffen them; beat them well together, and place in the bottom of a hot entrée dish; place the scollops in a circle on the top, and with a spoon place the mushrooms in the centre, and pour the sauce round; sprinkle the scollops lightly with finely-chopped parsley and grated Parmesan cheese mixed together, and serve.

SALMIS OF SNIPES.

Take six snipes, lightly roast them, cut them in halves, lay each half on a piece of toasted bread the same size, and keep very hot; make a sauce as follows: One pint of stock, a few allspice, two bay-leaves, a blade of mace, a piece of onion and celery, some seasoning boiled together ten minutes; thicken with a little roux, add two glasses of sherry and a little soy, and strain through a fine hair sieve; dish the halves of snipe on the toast in a circle overlapping one another, and pour the boiling sauce over them, and serve.

TO ROAST THREE WIDGEON.

Place them in a baking-tin covered with buttered paper, and bake for thirty minutes; serve on a very hot dish with some gravy thickened with roux, and well seasoned and colored with a little soy and some port wine poured over them.

TO ROAST THREE WOODCOCKS.

Lay the woodcocks on rounds of toasted bread to catch the trail, cover with buttered paper, and bake twenty-five minutes in a hot oven; serve with the same gravy as the widgeon.

CHEESE REMEQUINS.

Boil half a pint of milk, add four ounces butter and some seasoning; when the butter is melted, add four ounces flour and stir over the fire until the paste leaves the sides of the stewpan quite free; let it get nearly cold, then stir in five eggs and five ounces grated Parmesan cheese and a pinch of sugar; fill the paper cases with the mixture, and bake twenty minutes; dish them on a napkin, and serve immediately they come out of the oven.

ICE PUDDING A LA CINTRA.

Boil six ounces well-washed rice in a quart of milk until quite tender, add a gill of cream, six ounces powdered white sugar, half a glass of noyeau, six eggs well whisked together over a slow fire until boiling; stand the stewpan immediately in cold water, keep stirring until nearly cold. This custard must now be placed in a freezer used for making ices, and well worked with a spatula until thoroughly frozen; fill a mould with the ice and bed it in rough ice and salt, and place away until wanted. While the above process is going on, pare and quarter eight good oranges, place them in a sugar-boiler with one pint of water and one and a-half pounds sugar; allow the oranges to boil up in this gently for two minutes, then drain them on a sieve. Boil the syrup down to one-half of its original quantity, then add half a pound of apricot jam and a glass of noyeau, mix well together, and boil one minute; then pour it over the oranges, and let get quite cold. When about to send the pudding to table, dip the mould in lukewarm water; wipe with a clean cloth, turn the pudding out in a dish, and place the orange of compote round it, and serve.

PUNCH JELLY.

Dissolve two ounces gelatine in one pint and a-half of water, add the juice of two lemons and four ounces sugar, stand on the stove and let thoroughly melt; then add two whites of eggs whisked up in a gill of water, bring to the boil, and let stand two minutes; then pass through a jelly-bag, pouring back two or three times, until quite bright; add to it, when clear, half a glass of rum, the same of brandy and sherry, pour in the mould and let set. When wanted, dip the mould in warm water for twenty seconds, wipe with a cloth, and turn out in a silver or glass dish; garnish with some natural flowers.

STRAWBERRY CREAM.

Well whisk up half a pint of good cream, add to it three ounces powdered white sugar and the juice of half a lemon, mix three tablespoonfuls of strawberry jam in a little cold water, and strain it through a fine hair sieve.

COMPOTE OF FRENCH PLUMS.

Boil four ounces rice in a pint of milk until tender, add four ounces sugar and half a gill of cream, and one-half ounce isinglass dissolved in a little hot milk, pour into a border mould and let set; boil one pound sugar in a pint of water for five minutes, throw in one pound French prunes, and let boil ten minutes, color the syrup with a few drops of cochineal, and set away to get cold; dip the border in warmwater, and turn out; put the stewed plums in the centre and the syrup round, then it is ready for table.

COMPOTE OF PEARS.

Pare and core eight cooking-pears, place them in a stewpan with half a pint of water and two pounds sugar, four cloves, and a small piece of cinamon and a piece of lemon-peel, boil until the pears are tender, then strain the syrup, color red with cochineal and lay in the pears; let get cold; dish up in a glass dish with a little plain whipped cream on the top.

CLEAR MACARONI SOUP.

Ingredients: five pound lean beef, two onions, two carrots, one head of celery, one bay-leaf, a few allspice, pepper and salt, a little soy, three quarts of water, four ounces macaroni. How to use them: Cut up the carrots, onions, and celery into pieces, lay them in the bottom of a stewpan, and place the beef, cut into small pieces, on the top, sprinkle a little salt over it, and stand on the stove in a hot place to cook (taking care not to burn it) for one hour; then add three quarts of cold water, take off the fat, and boil it, take off all the scum, add a little soy, one bay-leaf, and a few allspice, and let simmer for three hours; strain through a cloth, and with a piece of paper laid lightly on the top of the soup take off any remaining fat. Boil four ounces macaroni in plenty of water until tender, then cut it into small pieces and place in the soup; bring it to the boil, and it is ready.

A LA REINE SOUP.

Ingredients: three pounds knuckle of veal, one onion, one carrot, a small piece of celery, two blades of mace, two ounces rice, one ounce sweet-almonds, a little roux, one quart of milk, two quarts of water and a gill of cream and seasoning. How to use them: Cut up the veal, onion, carrot and celery, and place in a stewpan with two quarts of water, add some pepper and salt, two blades of mace, and two ounces rice; boil all together three hours; strain off the liquor, and to it add one quart of milk and one ounce blanched sweet almonds, pounded fine in a mortar; boil and thicken with a little roux, strain through a fine hair sieve, add a gill of cream, and the soup is prepared.

ROUX FOR THICKENING ALL KINDS OF SOUPS, SAUCES, GRAVIES, ETC.

Ingredients: One pound good butter, fine flour. How to use them: Place the butter in a stewpan, bring it to the boil on the stove, taking care it does not burn; stand on one side to allow the sediment to settle, take off the scum, pour the clarified portion into a clean stewpan, to which add sufficient flour to make it into a stiff paste; place it on the stove in not too hot a place for about four hours, stirring occasionally until the roux assumes a fine golden color; put this away in a cool place, and it will keep good for weeks.

SOLES À LA CARDINAL.

Ingredients: Three soles filleted, half a pint of stock-broth, pepper and salt, the juice of one lemon, one glass of sherry, a little anchovy sauce and three drops of cochineal, a little roux, and two ounces butter. How to use them: Wipe the fillets with a clean cloth, sprinkle some pepper and salt over them, roll them up in the form of corks, place in a baking-tin with a little butter and the juice of a lemon, cover with a piece of buttered paper, and bake for fifteen minutes in a hot oven; when cooked dish them in a circle and pour over them a sauce made as follows: half a pint of stock, a little anchovy sauce, some seasoning, and a little roux boiled together; strain the sauce and add one glass of sherry and three drops of cochineal to color it pink.

TURBOT AND LOBSTER SAUCE.

Ingredients: One turbot, one lobster, half a pint of stock, a tablespoonful of anchovy sauce, a little cayenne pepper, and a little roux. How to use them: Wash the turbot, wipe it dry, and prick it all over with a large needle; then rub it over with the juice of a lemon and a little salt, place it in a fish-kettle, add sufficient cold water to cover the fish, then throw in a good handful of salt and set the turbot on the fire to boil; take off the scum, and let it gently boil for half an hour, more or less, according to the size of the fish; when the turbot is cooked lift it out of the water with the drainer, and slip it carefully on to a dish prepared to receive it; decorate it with lemon and parsley, and serve with a boat of lobster sauce.

Lobster Sauce: Boil half a pint of stock, add to it a tablespoonful of anchovy sauce, a little cayenne pepper, thicken with a little roux, and strain; add the meat of the lobster cut up into nice-size pieces.

FILLET OF BEEF À LA FINANCIERE.

Procure about five-pound fillet of beef, trim it, and lard it with fat bacon; cut up one onion, one carrot, and a small head of celery into a stewpan; add two blades of mace, a few allspice, two bay-leaves, a bunch of sweet herbs, and a little parsley; then lay in the fillet, add a pint of stock and some seasoning, cover with buttered paper, and bring to the boil on the stove; then place the stewpan in the oven for two hours; take off the paper when nearly cooked to allow the top to become crisp.

Sauce for the Fillet: Place in the stewpan one pint of stock, one onion, one-half pound lean bacon, a blade of mace, and a few allspice; boil forty minutes, take out the bacon, and thicken the gravy with a little roux; add a little soy, and strain the sauce; cut up the bacon into small squares, throw them into the sauce, add a tin of preserved mushrooms, place the fillet on a hot dish, glaze the top, and put the sauce round; serve very hot.

FOWLS À LA MACEDOINE.

Into a stewpan put one quart of stock, a blade of mace, one onion, and one carrot cut up, a piece of celery, a sprig of thyme, and some seasoning; lay in three small or two large fowls, prick them all over the breast with a needle; bring them to the boil and simmer thirty-five minutes; when cooked, pour the gravy from them into another stewpan; thicken it with a little roux; add a glass of port wine; strain it, and add a tin of macedoine vegetables; place the the fowls on the dish, glaze the breasts, and pour the sauce round them; place four small heaps of Brussels sprouts round them for garnish; serve very hot.

OYSTERS IN CASES.

Scald two dozen oysters in their own liquor, strain the liquor into a stewpan, add half a pint of milk, a little grated nutmeg and some seasoning; boil it, thicken with a little roux, put two oysters into each (ramequin case), and pour the sauce equally over all; sprinkle the tops with a few breadcrumbs, and bake in a hot oven ten minutes; dish in a circle on a napkin in a hot entrée-dish, garnish with parsley and serve.

MUTTON CUTLETS À LA SOUBISE.

Procure eight bones of small mutton, take off the chinebone and cut out twelve cutlets; into a stewpan put one onion, one carrot, and a piece of celery cut up, lay the cutlets in a circle, with the bone ends to the centre, on the top of the vegetables; add one quart of stock broth and some seasoning, and let gently simmer one hour; let the cutlets get cold in the liquor, then take them out and trim them; lay them in a sauté-pan, strain the liquor, and reduce it over a sharp fire to a demi-glaze; pour it over the cutlets, and when required, place the sauté-pan in a hot oven for ten minutes; boil eight onions in some stock until reduced to a pulp, add one ounce butter, a pinch of sugar, and strain through a coarse-mesh metal strainer, and bring it to the boil; dish the cutlets in a circle overlapping one another; pour the subise in the centre and the demi-glaze round them, and serve very hot.

GALANTINE OF VEAL.

Take from four pounds to five pounds breast of veal, take out bones, well beat it with the rolling-pin, and pick it all over with a fork, cover it with a layer of forcemeat, lay on it strips of fat bacon, hard-boiled eggs, gherkins, and mushrooms; roll it up, and tie tightly in a cloth, and boil it in the pot with the turkey for two hours; when cooked, press it between two dishes until cold.

CRUST FOR THE PIES.

Two pounds fine flour, one pound butter well rubbed in the flour, add two eggs and a little water, make into a compact paste, and let lay whilst you cut up the game and meat for the perigord pie.

THE GAME PIES.

Line two small French pie-tins, with the crust not too thick; cover the sides and bottom with forcemeat, cut up the game, whatever it may be, and fill the mould; cover the top of the meat with forcemeat, and then cover with a crust of the paste, wash over with egg, ornament to fancy with leaves and flowers, and bake in moderate oven for two hours; when cooked, fill up the pie with gravy from the pot the galantines were cooked in, adding a little gelatine to stiffen the gravy; place the pie in a cool place.

PERIGORD PIE.

Line a half-quartern bread tin with buttered paper, then a lining of the paste, cover the sides and bottom with forcemeat, sprinkle over with chopped mushrooms, then fill up the inside with strips of veal, bacon, and any cold chicken or turkey you may chance to have in the larder, a few truffles, a little grated nutmeg, pepper and salt, cover the meat over with forcemeat, and then a paste crust, wash over with egg-wash, and bake for two hours in a moderate oven; when baked, fill up the pie with gravy in which a little gelatine has been dissolved. Let the pie get cold, then cut out in nice square pieces, not too thick.

JELLIES.

Soak your gelatine thoroughly before using. To three-fourth pound opaque gelatine add six quarts of water; let soak for a good half hour. Now proceed to make the jelly: Take the gelatine, which will have swollen pretty freely by this time, and stand it on the side of the stove, add three pounds loaf-sugar, the juice of ten lemons, a small piece of cinamon; stir these ingredients well together until the gelatine and sugar are thoroughly dissolved, then take five whites of eggs, whisk up in a little water, then add them to the gelatine, and bring steadily to the boil. After it has stood a few minutes pass through a flannel jelly-bag; by pouring back some of the first through two or three times it will come as clear as crystal, and be ready to receive the flavors and color required for table. In ornamenting the moulds for the jellies care must be taken to blend the colors artistically; for example, a dark-colored jelly or cream would require ornamenting with white whipped jelly and light-colored fruits; and a light colored jelly or cream should have a dark-colored jelly or fruit to ornament it.

WHIPPED JELLY.

Whipped jelly being the principal ornamentation of most jellies and creams, can easily be made by taking about half a pint of warm clear jelly, and standing the basin containing it in a larger vessel of cold water or ice, and well whisking the jelly with a wire whisk until nearly cold. We will now proceed to ornament the moulds required for the jellies. For the *orange jellies,* pour about a wineglassful of clear jelly in the top of each mould, and strew a few preserved cherries and blanched pistachio nuts in it, stand it in ice-water to get cold quickly; when that is set, run in a layer of white whipped jelly, about one inch thick, and when that is set, fill up the mould with the orange jelly a little at a time, taking care not to put it in too hot, and only a small quantity at a time.

ORANGE JELLY.

Take enough clear jelly to fill the moulds required, add the juice of three oranges, also the yellow rind of the oranges rubbed on sugar, and the juice of one lemon; mix these well together, and strain through a muslin.

CHERRY JELLIES.

Pour a little clear jelly in the top of each mould, and with a spoon mix a sheet of gold leaf (which can be procured from the grocers) well in the jelly in each mould; let it set, then run in on the top of it a layer of white whipped jelly; when that is set, fill up with the cherry jelly, made as follows: Take enough clear jelly to fill the moulds, add one glass of noyeau and a few drops of cochineal to color it.

WINE JELLY.

Ornament the top of the mould with a little clear jelly, in which drop some green grapes and a few preserved cherries; then, when that is set, run a layer of whipped jelly, colored pink with a few drops of cochineal, on the top of the first layer, and when that is set fill up the mould with the wine jelly, made as follows: To one pint of clear jelly add a glass of sherry and brandy mixed.

CLEAR JELLY.

Ornament the top of the mould with a little clear jelly, colored pink; when that is set, run in a layer of white whipped jelly; when that is thoroughly cold, fill up the mould with the clear jelly a little at a time.

Now ornament six moulds for the creams.

TWO PINEAPPLE CREAMS.

Run a little clear jelly in the top of each mould; when that is set, run a layer, about half an inch thick, of whipped jelly, colored red with cochineal.

ONE NOYEAU CREAM.

Run in the top of the mould a layer of white whipped jelly.

ONE VANILLA CREAM.

Run in the top of the mould a little clear jelly and a few green grapes.

TWO LEMON CREAMS.

Run in the top of each mould a little clear jelly; in one put some preserved cherries, in the other a little gold leaf; when set, run in a layer of whipped jelly, colored red with cochineal.

HOW TO BOIL A HAM.

If the weight of the ham is about ten pounds it will require three hours and a-half gentle boiling. Soak the ham for a few hours, then scrape it clean, and saw off the knuckle, place it in a stewpan, with a pinch of moist sugar, a blade of mace, a few allspice, and a sprig of thyme, cover it with cold water and boil as directed; leave it in the liquor to get cold, then take off the rind, wipe with a clean cloth, and cover it with rasped breadcrumbs.

HOW TO BOIL TONGUE.

Well wash a good pickled tongue and place it in a stewpan, cover with cold water, cut up one small onion and half a carrot, and a little celery, and a few allspice; throw these in the water with the tongue, and boil it until cooked (about three hours) which can easily be seen by running a fork in the centre; if it seems tender it is done; when cooked, throw it in cold water and take off the skin.

ASPIC JELLY.

How to make: Take the liquor the galantines were boiled in, take off the fat, and pour the clear portion into a stewpan, and to each quart of the liquor add two ounces gelatine, one onion, one carrot, a little celery, two ounces lean ham, and a small bunch of herbs, a blade of mace, and a few allspice, pepper and salt; stand the stewpan on the stove, occasionally stirring, until the gelatine is melted, then add five whites of eggs well whisked in a little cold water, stir all together, and bring gently to the boil; take off the stove and let stand five minutes, pass through a flannel jelly-bag, putting back some of the aspic as it runs through two or three times, then it will be quite ready for using for the Russian salads, eel in aspic and the savory aspic.

RUSSIAN SALAD.

How to make: Procure carrots, onions, turnips, and potatoes, boil them, cut them into small square pieces and let them get cold; also have a beet-root cut up, and some preserved green peas; place these vegetables in small groups (arranging the different colors fancifully) in a mould having a hollow centre, fill up the mould with the vegetables, then fill in on the vegetables some nearly cold aspic jelly, and place away to set; when turned out of the mould, in the hollow in the centre put a little mayonaise sauce and a few small pieces of lobster.

EEL IN ASPIC.

How to make: Procure a boned eel, weighing about one pound, from the fishmonger's; with a knife take out any small bones that may be by chance left in, sprinkle some pepper and salt and a little chopped parsley over it, and roll it up, tie in a piece of muslin, and boil twenty minutes in water to which a little vinegar has been added; let it get thoroughly cold, cut it into slices, and place the best round the sides of the mould, and the rough pieces in the centre, fill up the mould with nearly cold aspic jelly; place in the larder until wanted.

SAVORY ASPIC.

How to make: Cut up some pieces of cooked veal and ham and a few preserved mushrooms, the whites of two hard-boiled eggs. Take a plain mould, run in the top a little aspic jelly, place in the aspic jelly a little parsley in small sprays, a piece of beetorot, and some cooked white of hard-boiled egg; work these in some fancy shape, then let set, and fill up the mould with the meat, and fill in with nearly cold aspic jelly, and place in the larder until wanted.

PUFF PASTE.

Ingredients: one pound flour, one pound good butter, one egg, one lemon. How to use them: Put the flour on the pastry-slab, rub in one ounce butter, make a hole in the centre, in which put one egg and the juice of one lemon, mix it with cold water into a smooth, flexible paste, and dry up with a little flour and let it lie ten minutes on the slab, take the fifteen ounces butter, and with a large knife work out the water from it, bringing it to the same consistency as the paste, upon which place, press it out with the hand, then fold over the edges of the paste so as to hide the butter, and roll it with the rolling-pin to the thickness of a quarter of an inch, thus making it nearly two feet in length; fold over one third then fold over the other third, thus making a square, place it with the ends top and bottom before you, shaking a little flour over and under it, and repeat the rolls and turns twice as before. Flour a board or tin, upon which lay the paste, and put it in some cool place for half an hour; then roll it twice more, turning it as before; let it lie another quarter of an hour, give it two more rolls, making seven in all, and it is ready for use when required.

SHORT PASTE.

Ingredients: one pound flour, one-half pound butter, the yolk of one egg, and a little water. How to use them: Rub the butter well in the flour, make a hole in the centre, break in the yolk of one egg, and mix into a smooth, compact paste with cold water, then it is ready for use.

SWISS PASTRY.

Take a piece of short paste, roll it out the thickness of a penny-piece, spread some marmalade thinly over it, then cover it with a layer of paste the same thickness; wash the top over with egg, and sprinkle over it some chopped almonds and coarse white sugar; mark with a knife nice-size pieces, and bake it in a brisk oven.

MINCE PIES.

Mincemeat, how to make. Ingredients: One pound currants, one pound sultanas, one-half pound beef suet, one-half pound moist sugar, two pounds apples, one pound mixed peel, one-quarter ounce mixed spice, the grating and juice of one lemon and one orange. How to use them: Well wash and pick the currants and sultanas; chop up the suet very fine, using the sugar to separate it; pare the peel off, and take out the cores of the apples, and chop them moderately fine; chop up the mixed peel very fine, sprinkle the spice over the ingredients, and well mix together; grate the rind of the orange and lemon over it, and add the juice of the lemon and orange; place in stone jars, and it will keep good for months in a cool place. Line the bottom of some small patty-pans with a thin cover of short paste; place a little heap of mincemeat in the centre, then sprinkle a little water over them with a brush, and cover the tops with puff-paste about a quarter of an inch thick, and bake in a good oven. When baked, sprinkle a little powdered white sugar over them, and be sure to take them out of the pans while they are warm, because if let get cold, they will stick to the bottom, and tear the short paste and let out the mincemeat. Warm the mince pies previously to dishing up, as they should not be quite cold when eaten.

FOR ITALIAN PASTRY AND TIPSY CAKE.

Ingredients: One pint milk, six ounces loaf sugar, five eggs, a small piece of cinnamon. Boil the milk, sugar, and cinnamon together, whisk the eggs well up, pour the boiling milk over them, well whisking all the time, stir them well together over a slow fire until boiling; take off and stand the stewpan in cold water and stir until cold.

ITALIAN PASTRY.

Take some short paste, roll out very thin, spread some custard over it, cover it with a layer of short paste, then mask the top over with meringue, made as follows: Four whites of eggs beaten to a stiff froth, stir in five ounces powdered white sugar, bake it in a cool oven; when baked, cut it up in fancy shapes, and ornament the tops with preserved fruits.

MERINGUES.

Ingredients: Eight whites of eggs, one pound powdered white sugar. Break the whites of eggs very carefully into a clean pan; then with a wire whisk beat them to a stiff snowy froth, so that the whisk will stand upright in them; then gently stir in the sugar, and with a dessertspoon lay out in little heaps like half eggs on stiff white paper, sprinkle a little powdered sugar over them, and bake in a very cool oven; when baked a nice light brown, take out and lift up the meringue, and with a teaspoon scoop out the soft part in the centre and place back in the oven to dry for a few minutes. Keep in a dry place until wanted. Before sending to table fill in the hollows with whipped cream, and place two together so as to form an egg in shape.

SANDWICH PASTRY.

Cut out of a sheet of puff-paste strips about three inches long, an inch wide, and about half an inch thick; lay them on their edge and bake in a hot oven; when nearly cooked, sprinkle some fine sugar over them; when cooked spread some jam on one piece and cover it with another, the same as a sandwich.

THE AMATEUR PAINTER.

A Manuel of Instruction in the Arts of

Painting,

Varnishing

AND

Gilding,

With Plain Rules for the practice of every department of HOUSE AND SIGN Painting.

CONTENTS:

Colors and How to Mix them. Compound Colors. Oils, Varnishes. Polishes. Gilding Materials. Miscellaneous Materials. Grinding and Washing Colors. Cleanliness in Working. Practice of Painting. Practice of Varnishing and Polishing. Practice of Gilding. Instructions of Sign Writing. Harmony of Colors. Birds-Eye Maple in Distemper. Satin Wood. Mahogany in Distemper. Mahogany in Oil. Rose Wood.

This book is thorough in detail in every branch of Painting. By its aid every man can become his own Painter, in whatever kind of work he desires to undertake. PRICE 25 CENTS.

RIDDLES, CONUNDRUMS AND PUZZLES.

We believe in making home happy, and whatever tends to promote this condition we welcome with joy. This book is chock full of the choicest, newest and best collection of

Riddles, Charades, Enigmas, Puzzles, Rebusses, Conundrums, Anagrams, Transpositions, Paradoxies, Acrostics, Problems,

and other entertaining matter ever put together within the covers of any book heretofore published. It is a real live, inscrutible SPHINX, as inscrutible and mysterious as the fabulous Egyptian one of old.

There is fun for the Mirthful, food for the Curious, and matter for the Thoughtful in abundance, Price 20 Cents.

FORTUNE-TELLING

MADE EASY,

And the Witche's Key to Lucky Dreams.

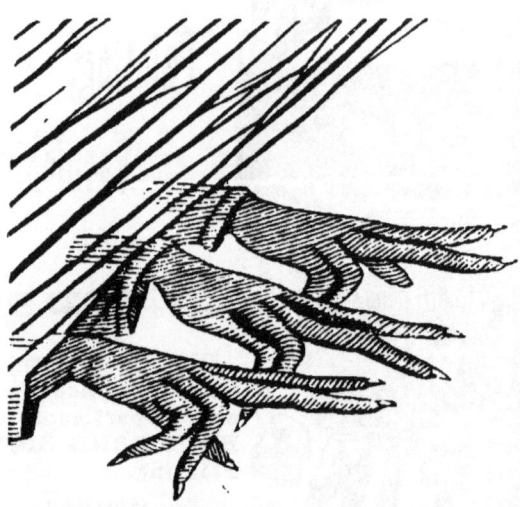

Every person their own Fortune Teller. With this book you can tell your own or any person's fortune far better than any astrologer, clairvoyant or medium can for you. It foretells exactly what will happen to you in the future; it gives the Hindoo Secrets of Love, and how to manage, what to say, and what to do to gain the affections, the love, the heart and the hand of the person you desire to marry; it gives the Art of Telling Fortune by the Lines of the Hand; it contains a Complete Dictionary of Dreams, so that you can at once interpret any dream as soon as you hear it. It tells you a Charm to Protect you from Danger. It teaches how to make the Lucky Dream Rose. Who your Husband or your Wife shall be. The Love Charm. How to Know the Sex of Children before Birth. To know how soon you will Marry. To know what Fortune you will have. The Lover's Charm. The only true method to tell Fortunes by Tea or Coffee Cup. To know if your love of a person will be mutual. Fortune Telling by Cards. What you will be successful in. What your absent Wife or Husband is doing. What your Fortune Destiny is. Whether your Wife, Husband or Intended is **true to you.** Whether you will ever Marry or not. Whether you will have money left you. How to be successful in your love affairs. Whether you will be a Widow. Whether you will die Rich or Poor. Seven Signs of Speedy Marriage. Signs how to Choose a good Husband or Wife. In fact there is no end to the mysterious revelations. You can foretell the Results of all Commercial and Business Speculations. It points out clearly the path to prosperity, Riches and Happiness. If you have encountered losses, misfortune or treachery of friends, or have been slighted by the one your affections have centered upon, or had bad luck in life, Old Gypsy Madge will help you through, and tell you how to **conquer at last.** She'll teach you to overcome all obstacles and turn the tide of Good Luck towards you. Sample copy and terms to Agents sent by mail, post paid, for 25 cents, or five copies to one address for $1.00.

Address E. G. RIDEOUT & CO., Publishers,

10 BARCLAY STREET, N. Y.

Ball-Room Dancing

WITHOUT THE AID OF A MASTER, AND BALL-ROOM MANUAL.

DANCING, as an elegant accomplishment, has ever stood prominent, because no other art or exercise can give the individual that graceful demeanor and easy deportment so essential to a correct appearance in cultured society. As it is not always convenient to have recourse to a teacher of dancing, this work aims to supply the deficiency. In this it has been very successful. By a series of practical and lucid instructions the art of dancing is so simplified that any one can become proficient in the art Without the Aid of a master. In addition to specific detailed instructions as to how to dance, it gives some very valuable information relating to Organizing a Ball, Ball-Room Toilet, Etiquette of the Ball-Room. All the Popular Dances are given, and the whole is illustrated by numerous cuts and diagrams, making the art so simple that the most ignorant can become experts in it

Price 25 Cents.

LOVE MAKING;

Or An Easy Road to Marriage.

Start right and the battle is half won. A man in love, or a lady whose heart has been touched with the burning fire of true love, will find in in this book strange secrets that no friend could tell them, and an **Easy Way to Mariage through Love's intricate pathway**. It also contains many Ancient Hidden Secrets that the married should know. If a wife has a wayward husband, or feels that she is neglected, get this book into his hands at once, and it will surely reclaim him to his first love. It startles while it teaches. It proves that the Way to Win is no longer a secret. If you follow this writer's advice, failure to win the object of your choice is impossible. Send for this book. It will pay you a thousand times the price. Every country, civilized and barbarous has been ransacked to get **The Secrets of Love Making**. It will bring joy to thousands of both sexes, and cause more hearts and hands to be united in marriage than all other instrumentalities combined. It is full of **strange things** regarding Love Making which you never heard before. If you are in love, and it is not reciprocated, this Great Book will open wide Love's barred door for you, and break down every barrier. Sample copy and terms to Agents sent by mail, post paid, for **25 cents**, or five copies to one address for $1.00.

Address E. G. RIDEOUT & CO., Publishers,

10 BARCLAY STREET, N. Y.

JOLLY TIT BITS FOR MIRTHFUL MORTALS.

"Too Funny for Anything."

Josh Billings, Bret Harte and Mark Twain rolled into one. It is not to much to say that this book contains the Choicest Humor in the English Language. Its size is mammoth, containing more than One Thousand of the Raciest Jests, Comical Hits. Exhilarating Stories, Flowers of Wit, Excruciating Jokes, Uproarious Poems, Rollicking Songs, Laughable Sketches, Darky Comicalties, Clown's Efforts, Button-bursting Conundrums, Endmen's Jokes, Plantation Humor, Funny Caricatures, Hilalutin' Dialogues Kurieus Scenes, Kute Sayings, Ludicrous Drolleries, Peculiar Repartees In fact, it is a complete "Joe Miller" and "Tom Brown" in the one volume. All the Great Comic Stars refer to it, because they can find in it something to " touch the funny-bone" every time. It contains an immense collection of Irish Bulls, Dutch Comicalities, and Yankee Yarns, affording fun for a life-time. Humorously illustrated by lots of Komical Kuts.

Price 25 Cents.

LADIES' AND GENTLEMEN'S
LETTER-WRITER.

A complete Letter Writer for Ladies and Gentlemen. This book is not a collection of letters and examples, as is generally the case with all "Complete Letter Writers" now in use, but it is a book which actually tells how to write a letter, upon any subject, out of the writer's "own head." It gives much very necessary information relating to Punctuation, Spelling, Grammar, Writing for the Press, Legal Importance of Letters, Love, Courtship and Marriage. It also contains the Art of Rapid Writing, by the abbreviations of Long-hand, and a Dictionary of Abbreviations. This book is worth its weight in gold to all. No one can fail to be benefitted by some of the information it contains. It contains all the points and features that are in other Letter Writers, with very much that is new, original and very important, and which cannot be got in any other book. Price by mail,

25 Cents.

Address E. G. RIDEOUT & CO., Publishers,

10 BARCLAY STREET, N. Y.

THE HORSE-OWNER'S GUIDE,

AND COMPLETE
HORSE-DOCTOR.

There is no one who owns, cares for or works a horse, who can afford to be without this work. It is just the handy, complete and practical manual that has long been needed by horse owners. It is written by a well-known Veterinary Surgeon and Horse Dealer of great experience, so that no matter of importance relating to the horse in all its existence is neglected. This work thoroughly informs you about

THE KIND OF HORSE TO BUY. TO DETECT HORSE JOCKEY-TRICKS. TO MANAGE A HORSE. TO SHOE A HORSE. TO BREAK AND TRAIN HORSES. TO CURE ALL KINDS OF HORSE DISEASES.

THERE IS NOTHING RELATING TO

BUYING, BREEDING, REARING, TRAINING, SHOE-ING, FEEDING, TAMING, BREAKING AND DOCTORING HORSES

but is thoroughly detailed. In addition is given the **Art of Training and Taming Horses** by a new method. And it tells--How to make a Horse lie down.—To Catch a Wild Horse.—To Teach a Horse to Pace.—To Make a Horse Stand.—To Make a Horse Sit on its Haunches.—To Make a Horse Come Down for Mounting.—To Make a Horse Follow you.—To Make a Horse Stand Still without Hitching.—To Break Horses to Ride.—To Prevent a Horse Running Away. Illustrated with Engravings

This Great Practical Work on the Horse is only 25 Cents.

THE SARA BERNHARDT
BOOK OF BEAUTY.

Ladies' and Gentlemen's Toilet Companion. How to Become Beautiful.

Cures for all diseases affecting the personal appearance. All the valuable recipes of the world. How to attain Bodily Vigor, Physical Development. Beauty of Feature and Symmetry of Form, with the Science of Dressing with Taste, Elegance and Economy. To those to whom nature has been sparing in its gifts suggestions are here offered that will enable them to overcome these defects, and become beautiful, elegant and graceful, and to be admired and sought after by the opposite sex. Among the numerous other matters it tells. How to Improve the Complexion. Make Cosmetics. Remove Freckles. Make the Eyes Beautiful. Cause the Eyelashes and Brows to Grow Long. Prevent the Hair Falling Off. Prevent Grey Hair, Cause the Beard and Mustache to Grow. Cure Baldness. Remove Superfluous Hair. Preserve the Teeth. Cure Toothache. Have White Hands, Cure Corns. Cure Pimples. Invigorate the System. Increase the Memory. Prolong Life. Cure Nervous Ailments. Increase the Vital Forces. Produce Physical Vigor, etc. It gives a vast amount of other equally important information which cannot be enumerated here. Illustrated. Price by mail, post paid. **25 cents.**

E. G. RIDEOUT & CO., Publishers, 10 Barclay St., N. Y.

Parlor Magic or Stage Conjuring.
A COMPLETE WIZARD'S GUIDE.

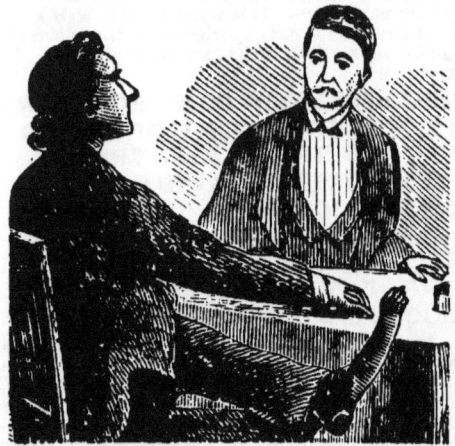

The Art of Conjuring Unveiled. As performed by the Wonderful Magicians, Houdin, Colonel Stodare, Heller, Wyman, and others. Comprising all their best Stage Tricks and giving Full Explanations for Performing them in the parlor or on the stage. These Tricks are elegantly Illustrated, thereby making them much easier to perform, and teaches the reader how to be a Magician without any further instructions. Any person can study this book a short time and perform the most difficult trick done by the best magicians. You can bring Bowls of Goldfish from an Empty Handkerchief; or Tell a Card by Smelling it, or Make a Card Vanish from the Pack and be found in a Person's Pocket; to make a Card Rise bodily out of a Pack; to Make a Marked Dime fly into the Centre of an Apple; to Make a Coin Answer Questions; to make it Shower Real Money; to Make a Handkerchief Change into an Egg: to Take several Bird Cages from a Hat; to Take Borrowed Rings and Live Doves out of an Omelet; the Chinese Solid Ring Trick; to Make Fresh Flowers Grow out of an Empty Flower Pot; the Flying Glass of Water; to Pull Several Live Rabbits out of a Hat, and then Roll them all into one; it teaches the Wonderful Sphinx Illusion Trick. This trick is worth a hundred dollars. The Cabinet of Skeletons and Spirits. The Indian Basket Trick is a fortune to an Amateur. To Make a Drum hang to the ceiling, Tap or Roll; to Make a Living Woman Sleep in Mid Air. The above are a few among many of the wonderful tricks that this book teaches how to perform. Persons desiring to give an entertainment, either in a parlor or hall, can learn enough from this book to delight a company for two hours. These tricks are the very best ever performed. One thousand dollars a night has been received at the door to see these tricks performed. Sample copy and terms to Agents, sent by mail, post paid, for **25 cents.**

READY-MADE AUTOGRAPH ALBUM VERSES.

As everybody wishes to oblige his lady friends, here is the very book that must be acceptable to everybody. Expressive of almost every human feeling and sentiment, such as Love, Friendship, Respect, Admiration, Good Wishes, etc., including a great number of Acrostics for Proper Names, all entirely original. No gentleman, young, middle-aged or old, can go at all into society without having some fair lady's Book of Autographs plumped into his hands. He feels that to refuse would stamp him a downright bear. He must comply. Left to himself he would probably write "himself down as an ass." But this book will take him out of the dilemma. Here he will find something to write, at once eloquent and appropriate, to suit every phase of feeling, sentiment or humor. Any article that he may copy from this book will stamp him as a gentleman in the best meaning of the term.

Price 25 Cents.

Address E. G. RIDEOUT & CO., Publishers,
10 BARCLAY STREET, N. Y.

www.ingramcontent.com/pod-product-compliance
Lightning Source LLC
Chambersburg PA
CBHW032239080426
42735CB00008B/930